DOGS
Breeding & Showing

Dogs

BREEDING & SHOWING

Catherine G. Sutton

B. T. Batsford Ltd · London

By the same author:

Dog Shows and Show Dogs
The Observer's Book of Dogs
The Beagle
The Irish Wolfhound
The Afghan Hound
The Irish Setter
The Training and Care of the Family Dog
Beagles
Dog Shows Explained

ISBN 0 7134 4158 5

Photoset by Deltatype, Ellesmere Port
Printed by The Anchor Press Ltd,
Tiptree, Essex
for the Publishers
B. T. Batsford Ltd
4 Fitzhardinge Street
London W1H 0AH

Contents

*To all my very many canine friends throughout
the world, four-legged and human, who have helped
me gain the knowledge and experience without which
I could not have written this book.*

*The photographs were taken by Diane Pearce,
except in the few cases otherwise indicated.*

Introduction

The fascination of breeding and showing dogs is a real one; if done
properly the activity is time-consuming, demanding, and on occasions
heartbreaking, but it can be very rewarding too despite the financial
drain that so often accompanies it. Such a hobby, if that it be, should
only be pursued by those really dedicated to it and filled with a certain
amount of optimism. This is not a pursuit for the weak of heart, or those
not prepared to work all hours when Nature demands. It never was
easy to breed quality dogs as those who have run the course know only
too well. Nature is adept at dashing our hopes just when we think we
are conquering our disappointments and failures. Our hopes may be
raised, only to be frustrated with a future litter. As in everything else in
life, that little bit of luck is welcome; indeed in dog breeding and
showing it is not only welcome but necessary.

In over 30 years of breeding and showing dogs I have had my share of
success, but equally I have had failures; only if you are prepared to
learn from these failures will you ever make the top grade as a breeder.
There is no doubt that there is great pleasure and satisfaction to be
gained in breeding and showing dogs whatever your chosen breed; but
do remember also that there are disappointments and unhappy
moments that may make you feel that you should not go on. It is not all
plain sailing by any means. However, it is fascinating and in no time
you will find yourself thoroughly absorbed and involved once again. It
is difficult not to be, particularly if you decide to show the dogs you
have bred because you are proud of them—let us hope that the judges
will endorse your own opinion.

In this book I want to take you through the various stages that are
all-important to successful breeding and showing. There is no greater
thrill than to win in the show ring with stock that you have planned and
bred yourself. Money can buy most of our top dogs (not all), but I have
never had the same thrill in winning with stock that I have bought as
with stock that I have bred.

Initially, of course, one must buy and this purchase should be given a
very great deal of thought and should be the basis for your own stock

and one from which you are hoping to produce your champions.

If you are to achieve this you will need to know the very basic principles of genetics, how to whelp and rear puppies correctly, how to care for dogs and maintain your kennels in a good state of hygiene (of the utmost importance at all times)—and of course you will need to know about the world of dog shows and how they are run. I hope this book will give you the knowledge which will be the foundation of a successful breeding career, whether you live in the United Kingdom, the United States, or elsewhere.

May I wish you well in your endeavour to breed your first winner, then your first Champion; by the time you have achieved that aim, you will have succumbed to the fascination of breeding better dogs and you will be planning your next litter.

I

Breeding

1

The choice of a brood bitch

Most people decide to breed from their bitch as an after-thought. They probably bought her as a companion for the family and at the time of purchase had no intention of breeding from her. They may think that a litter would do her good or that it would be a marvellous education for their children to see Nature at work. Both these reasons are valid and acceptable and it is from these small beginnings that we can recruit many dog-breeders for tomorrow. However, many people have not already got a chosen breed and wish to acquire a bitch with the intention of breeding. It is most important that this choice be given a great deal of thought.

On page 145 you will find a list of breeds recognized in Britain by the Kennel Club. There are 124. There are also other breeds, which, for want of a better name, are recognized in Britain as 'Rare Breeds'. These do not, as yet, have enough registrations and/or entries at shows to warrant the granting of Challenge Certificates by the Kennel Club. They are usually entered in the Non-Classified Classes, although at the larger shows they may have their own separate breed classes. These rare breeds are marked in the list with an asterisk (*). In all, there are 154 breeds in the list, a marvellous selection, and they can all be seen at Championship Shows.

On page 149 is the list of breeds recognized by the American Kennel Club—there are some differences from the British list. Any breeds not on the list of those recognized in America are grouped under the heading 'Miscellaneous'.

What are the factors in your choice? Think carefully before choosing, because it would hardly be wise to buy one of those magnificent Irish Wolfhounds if you do not have enough accommodation, and if your purse is not full enough to provide all the food she will need, particularly when she is in whelp.

If you are embarking on a first-ever whelping venture you must

3

certainly choose a breed that is comparatively easy to whelp. Of course in every breed there can be unforeseen difficulties but there are breeds that do not usually have any problems. After experience with one of these breeds you can take your chance with a breed that is not perhaps renowned for ease of whelping.

Of course there are many other considerations that you should take into account. It may be that you want a bitch that will work, a gundog that will train to the gun, or a bitch that will train quickly in obedience. The choice must be yours but do give it very careful thought and always remember that you choose the bitch and she certainly does not choose you; you therefore bear some real responsibility.

As the bitch you choose is to be the basis of your breeding programme it would be well worth while to read any available book on the breed concerned. There are few breeds today that do not have a publication to tell you all about them. Go to the local dog show and talk to any breeders of your particular breed whom you may find there. If you have chosen one of the less common breeds it may be necessary for you to go to one of the bigger shows to make contact with the breeders.

For information on shows, contact your Kennel Club. Addresses and telephone numbers are given at the end of the book. The dog press will give you additional information on shows and breeders. In Britain, *Dog World* and *Our Dogs* are available from most newsagents.

The official magazine of the Kennel Club in Britain is the *Kennel Gazette*, which is available from the Club. The official magazine of the American Kennel Club, like the *Kennel Gazette* published monthly, is *Pure-Bred Dogs: American Kennel Gazette*. This is a very substantial publication, and contains details not only of all the actions taken by the American Kennel Club's Board of Directors, but also of the awards at all dog shows for the previous month plus field trials and obedience trials. It also lists all new Champions and approved obedience degree winners. Like the *Gazette* in Britain, it lists all future events. It is available from the American Kennel Club.

You will, of course, be buying your initial stock from a breeder, who will probably guide you as to your future programme. It is well worth while taking heed of the advice given by the breeder. There is a lot to learn about any particular breed; if you can gain advice and help from one much more experienced and knowledgeable than yourself it is very stupid not to take advantage of it, particularly if the breeder is reputable and successful. For instance, if you are buying a coated breed there are bound to be some strains that are known for growing better coats than others with a different pedigree. In other breeds where the carriage of the tail is very important some breeding lines will be known for their very good tail carriage and some for their not-so-good tail carriage. The same applies in breeds where perhaps the formation of the mouth is very important: if an incorrect mouth happens to appear, a breeder of experience could most likely pin-point where in the pedigree this bad mouth has come from. A breeder of experience in a particular breed should know his pedigrees inside-out and will have learned the hard way—by trial and error. If such a breeder is prepared to give you the benefit of his experience and help you in your future breeding programme, be ready to accept this help as it could save you valuable time and money.

Don't buy from the first kennel that you visit even if you do think that there is a puppy or adult there that would suit your purpose. By visiting several kennels you can get a very good idea of the standard of the kennel and its inmates and be able to assess the quality or otherwise of the stock offered.

Naturally you will want to purchase the best available animal that you can afford, and it may be that you wish to buy a show bitch that you can breed from at a later date. Do remember that it is not always the show bitches that produce the best puppies. So often the litter sister that is retained in the kennels proves a better producer than her more glamorous sister. Providing your bitch has no outstanding faults and is backed up by a good pedigree there is no reason why she should not produce good stock if put to the right dog.

It is a very grave mistake to think that any animal will do to breed with; this way you are certainly not giving yourself a fair chance as a breeder. It must never be forgotten that the bitch's faults will be transmitted to her offspring just as the dog's faults will be. They may not necessarily be apparent in the first generation but can be expected to appear in later generations. It is a fallacy to think that because a good stud dog is used all the puppies will be good ones. In fact many owners of stud dogs can be quite selective in respect of the bitches that they will accept for their stud dog, and who can blame them? It is absolutely essential that the brood bitch should be as near the standard of the breed as possible and that the ancestors throughout the pedigree should be free from outstanding faults as these very faults that should be eradicated have a strange habit of re-appearing without any warning.

Health and temperament are a very important consideration in the brood bitch. A nervous, shy, highly strung bitch must never be considered as a suitable brood. She should have an even temperament; although some breeds are permitted to be wary of strangers, she must never ever show any signs of viciousness or aggressiveness.

Depending on the breed, I like to see a brood bitch with a little extra length of loin plus a fair width. This allows adequate space for her puppies to develop and she is more likely to have an easy whelping with strong, live whelps.

In the toy breeds I feel it is asking for trouble to breed from very small bitches as the usual result is that your veterinary surgeon has to do a Caesarian. Experience has shown that it is much more sensible in the toy breeds to mate a larger bitch to a small dog. This should help to ensure that the puppies are small enough for the bitch to be able to whelp them naturally. Toy brood bitches, like their bigger sisters in other breeds, must be strong, fit and well. It is quite hopeless to use small, weedy specimens as broods. On the other hand, one must also remember that a true toy is small because it carries the genes which produce smallness and not necessarily because it has been badly reared and a weakling from birth.

The age at which a bitch is ready to be bred from varies with the breed. The toy breeds are ready to be bred from much sooner than their bigger sisters. No bitch should be bred from until she is fully mature and for the larger breeds this can be anything up to nearly three years. On the other hand it is advisable to breed from some of the toy breeds before the bones of the pelvis become too set and thus produce whelping problems.

The brood bitch should not be bred from more than once a year and even less often in the larger breeds. In deciding whether to mate a bitch at two successive seasons it is necessary to take into consideration the number of whelps she has successfully reared from her previous litter or litters. A bitch that is a big, strong example of the breed, has only reared a couple of puppies, and has lost no condition may quite safely be bred from again at her next season. On the other hand a bitch that has reared a good-sized litter for her particular breed should not be asked to produce for at least another year. A bitch that is overworked as a brood cannot be expected to produce top class healthy puppies. One's aim as a breeder is surely to produce good, healthy puppies, and never to use your bitch simply as a machine producing puppies that neither you nor she can be proud of.

A brood bitch, no matter what breed, should always be kept in the peak of condition, as if she is allowed to become fat and lethargic she will not be fit for her job; in many cases she will not come into season regularly and when mated will often miss. This is disappointing to all concerned and a waste of time and money. Don't let it happen: keep your bitch in hard condition with good food and regular exercise and avoid any unnecessary disappointment.

It is perhaps a common thought with laymen that to have a bitch and let her have puppies is a great way of making a few extra pennies. If you think along these lines do not take up dog-breeding. If your bitch was a well-bred puppy, sold as a pet, she might reasonably have been sold to you for £80 (US $150) depending on the breed. Add on the price of all the various inoculations. Prices vary, and some breeds may cost twice as much, or even more. It is unlikely that you will breed from your bitch, again depending on the breed, until she is about 14 months which means that you have probably kept her for at least a year and this would cost anything from over £100 (US $180) for the small-sized breeds to three times as much for the big ones. Add to this the stud fee when she is ready to be mated plus extra feeding whilst in whelp, the essential heating after the birth of the puppies plus, of course, the rearing of the whelps. You may be fortunate and have no troubles over the whelping: at the end of eight weeks your pups will be ready to go and you can cash in on your 'fat profit'. As a new breeder you will have to advertise your puppies in the dog press or local papers and so the profit gradually diminishes—until you finish up with quite a large hole in your pocket!

If you are unable to sell all your puppies, the longer you keep them the bigger drain they become on your pocket; in the end it could be that you decide to keep one simply because you could not sell it. This is not so significant in the smaller breeds but it certainly is in the large breeds that do need a lot of nourishment while they are growing. Financial profit is therefore far from assured. It is an undisputed fact that it is easier to build up a kennel than it is to cut it down, particularly with stock that is not quite top quality. It is therefore all the more essential to buy the best brood bitch that you can afford and be quite ruthless in choosing and keeping only the very best of her litters. If you do not think that any of the progeny are good enough do not be tempted to keep them. Each generation should be an improvement on the one before and only by very selective breeding can you hope to reach the top.

2

A breeding programme

The laws of heredity are generally well understood nowadays, and there is no reason why the breeding of livestock should be considered either a mystery or a lucky dip. All dog-breeders should take the trouble to understand the simple 'dominant' and 'recessive' Mendelian theory of genetics. There is not space here to explain it fully, but the most important idea to grasp is that, if two individuals are mated which are contrasting in any particular traits, one of these traits may appear in the offspring while the other does not. The trait which shows is known as 'dominant', while that which does not is known as 'recessive'. Where such a recessive trait is present in the genetic make-up of an individual, the individual will not breed pure, as far as that feature is concerned.

Gregor Mendel (1822–1884) was an Austrian monk who remained in his lifetime virtually unknown outside his own circle; it was not until nearly 20 years after his death that botanists were themselves reaching the conclusions he had come to in his life time. To explain the basics of his theory clearly, a certain amount of technicality is unavoidable. All living things are composed of cells. When a puppy is conceived, the sperm (from the male) and the ovum (from the female) unite to form one new cell, which becomes the new individual. In the centre of every cell is a nucleus, and when sperm and ovum unite, so do their respective nuclei. The new individual grows by division of the cell into two, four, eight and so on—all mature animals are made up of thousands of millions of cells.

The inheritance of all the characteristics that make up an individual is controlled by the nucleus of a cell. Inside the nucleus are the 'chromosomes'—generally 19 pairs of them. The genes for inherited characteristics are carried on the chromosomes, each gene having an opposite number on the paired chromosome. Each sperm cell and each ovum contains only one set of chromosomes; as the sperm and ovum fuse to form the new individual, these sets match up to form the pairs

8

already described. Therefore every new individual receives two sets of chromosomes, and therefore genes—one set from each parent. As cells divide (and so the animal develops), each individual chromosome splits lengthwise into identical halves; the two halves move to opposite ends of the cell, and then act in effect as full chromosomes, forming two new nuclei. The cell then divides fully; each new cell has a nucleus and therefore chromosome make-up identical with the parent cell. The genetic make-up of the individual animal is therefore laid down right at the beginning of its life—at the moment of conception.

Suppose the puppy receives, for a particular characteristic, a similar gene from each parent. In that case, that gene will be expressed visibly in the new puppy and the question of dominance and recessivity will not arise. The puppy is said to be *homozygous* for that feature, and in that respect will breed true.

What happens if the pair of genes differs—that is to say, if for a particular feature the puppy's inheritance from each parent differs? Back to Mendel. He did his early experiments with the aid of peas with long and short stems. Breeding long to long, they bred true, producing long-stemmed offspring. Short bred to short produced short offspring. When a long-stemmed plant was bred to a short-stemmed plant,

first cross

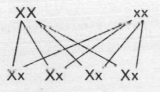

second cross

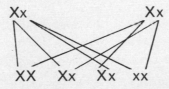

X = long-stemmed (dominant)
x = short-stemmed (recessive)

9

Mendel might have expected something in between. But the progeny were all long-stemmed, indistinguishable outwardly from their long-stemmed parents. *But*, when *this* generation of long-stemmed peas were bred to one another, they did not breed true, producing three long-stemmed offspring, roughly, to every short-stemmed. The diagram on page 9 explains why.

In this third generation, therefore, a quarter of the progeny are homozygous for long stems; in other words they will breed true for long stems like their long-stemmed grandparents; half of them are outwardly long-stemmed, but carry also the gene for short stems. In such cases the gene which is expressed visibly is said to be dominant; its counterpart, different and not outwardly expressed, is said to be recessive. Such individuals will not breed true for that characteristic, producing once again variable progeny. One quarter are, as you see in the diagram, homozygous for short stems, and will, like their short-stemmed grandparents, breed true for short stems if mated together.

Mendel worked with peas; but similar principles apply to dogs or any other animals. If a black Cocker Spaniel which is pure-bred for colour is mated to a red Cocker, also pure-bred for colour, the resulting litter will consist of black puppies only, black being dominant to red in this breed, just as the long-stemmed peas were dominant to the short-stemmed peas. If these cross-bred black Cockers are mated, brother to sister, their offspring will be some black and some red in the proportion of three black to one red. Of the blacks one third will breed true for black and the other two-thirds will breed black or red puppies according to how they are mated. The reds that are produced by the cross-bred blacks will breed as true for their colour as if no black ancestor had been introduced into their lineage at all. If a red Cocker bred in this way is mated to another red it will never sire or bear a black puppy. Neither will the pure dominant black Cocker ever produce a red puppy if it is mated to other blacks. The impure dominant blacks which are quite indistinguishable in colour from their pure dominant litter brothers or sisters will sire or produce a proportion of red puppies to certain mates. To understand this and the role of dominant and recessive genes is of the greatest importance to dog-breeders generally.

Recessive genes can skip one or several generations and will not appear unless there is an identical recessive gene coming from each parent. The heredity of a dog has therefore been likened to an iceberg because so little of an iceberg is above the surface of the water and by far the greater part is submerged. How true this is and how frustrating for the dog breeder on the occasions when all his carefully laid plans go astray!

For those who wish to delve further into the intricacies of genetics there are several very good books on it; but I have to add that unless one is prepared to know and admit to the faults in one's own animals it is no good even beginning to understand genetics. Kennel blindness, the inability to see the faults in one's own kennel, is perhaps the worst fault of all.

For all this a basic knowledge of genetics is important to the dog breeder or breeder of any livestock. In the past, it is true, good results have been obtained by those to whom the very word 'genetics' was unknown, but these breeders of by-gone days could have bred even better dogs with the knowledge now available. Occasionally a chance mating comes off but it is rare that stock bred on from such a chance mating is of any great merit. Breeders, or, should I say, genuine breeders, are all dedicated to breeding better stock and are proud to show and exhibit the results of a planned breeding programme. They are pleased to sell their stock abroad to win and be admired throughout the world.

Let us now look to the breeding programme.

Line breeding

This is the pairing up of two related animals but not so closely related as to entail inbreeding (see below). This is a fairly safe plan for amateurs to follow as it is a modification of the more risky inbreeding, producing much the same results, but not so quickly and perhaps less danger-ously. The object of line breeding is to have as close a relationship as possible to one or more animals of outstanding merit in the pedigree and here it is valuable to know as much as possible about the animals in a bitch's pedigree. Line-breeding demands the same high standards in the stock as are needed for the closer in-breeding. The pedigrees of animals used in line-breeding are more dissimilar than those in in-breeding and therefore a larger number of gene combinations must be expected to occur in the offspring. Genetic purity will take longer to establish. On the other hand, faults are less likely to be established and fixed. Line breeding can be considered a form of outcrossing, i.e. the breeding together of two animals that are unrelated, but naturally very much less drastic than a complete outcross. It is however quite wrong to think simply that in-breeding is 'dangerous' and that line-breeding is quite 'safe'. Line-breeding is probably the better method for the novice

11

breeder or a breeder who has only two or three bitches and is rather reluctant to mate animals which are too closely related.

In any breeding programme it is very important that the value of a particular dog or dogs should be recognized during their life time so that as many lines from them as possible among the descendants can be secured. If an animal appears on both sides of the pedigree and in more than one generation its influence will obviously be greater. This will ensure that a good degree of relationship to that animal is preserved. After its death breeding should continue to its best and nearest relative.

I have always felt it is rather unfortunate that we are not allowed to store away in a special bank at one of our Veterinary Colleges semen collected from some of our top dogs in various breeds. I know that in my own breeding programme I would have appreciated going back to one of my great dogs of the past. This is not possible at the moment and it is, therefore, all the more important that we make full use of our top dogs while they are still alive. Relationship is halved with each generation and when an animal only appears once on a pedigree its influence is not very strong, particularly when it appears four or five generations away.

Try to be aware of any recessive faults that may exist in your pedigree and never mate two animals that have the same common fault. Many breeders find that the mating of grandfather to grand-daughter is very successful, particularly if the line is known to be genetically clean. Niece to uncle can also be very useful and produce good results. If you intend to breed to the type of animal that you consider to be most representative of the breed standard it is essential that you line-breed fairly closely as the more distant the relationship, the more varied will be the type of puppies produced. Established dog-breeders should always be able to identify their puppies; there is nothing more pleasing to a dedicated breeder than to have litter after litter all of the same type. This shows for certain that the kennel is producing the type that the breeder considers fits the standard whether or not that type is correct in other people's eyes.

In-breeding
This is the mating of close relatives, father to daughter, mother to son, brother to sister etc. Some of the best stock in the world in livestock has been produced by in-breeding. Many laymen are horrified at the thought of such matings and pronounce it unnatural. This, of course, is quite untrue as it occurs among wild animals all the time.

When in-breeding, one must be aware of the faults and virtues of all

12

the animals in the pedigree and any puppies that do not come up to standard must be culled at birth. Haphazard in-breeding can only result in disaster and it could be that these disasters would not show until later generations. In-breeding can only be done successfully by rigorous culling in every generation of all specimens showing undesirable qualities or faults. In-breeding does not create either good or bad points. It will not introduce anything new into a strain but it will and can endorse good points just as it will emphasize bad points.

Many breeders never practise in-breeding. In fact they distrust it and claim that it does not work. This may be so for them but I feel that if they had persevered a little longer and selected their stock really rigorously success could have come their way as it has done for many others. However, these breeders seem to prefer the more gentle line-breeding and it is this method that I recommend to those who are about to plan their first litter. It may well be that if you have planned the first litter well, and the one after that, you will be on your way to producing your own strain of your chosen breed; then, you must not be afraid to in-breed to stabilise type further and gain genetic purity. In-breeding is satisfactory for all serious breeders.

Out-crossing

This is the mating of unrelated dogs and is the opposite of in-breeding. Out-crossing is usually carried out when a kennel has developed a strain and wishes to improve a particular point or to eradicate a fault or weakness. Unfortunately in doing this one can introduce faults that were not in the strain before, because the genetic make-up of the offspring of the mating will be unknown. Such an outcross mating can bring many problems and these may take several generations to get rid of. It is wiser to revert to line-breeding rather than risk the unknown in outcrossing.

The stud dog

Having decided to line-breed with your bitch you must study the pedigree very carefully. Never be tempted by the latest Champions in the breed. One so often hears the layman say that his dog or bitch's pedigree is as long as his arm and is full of Champions. Any pedigree can be as long as anybody's arm and there are Champions and Champions. Naturally Champions get more bitches sent to them than average dogs and therefore have a greater chance of throwing good stock. A good sire need not necessarily be a champion, but is a dog that is prepotent and throws top class stock to a variety of bitches and obviously has many highly desirable dominant genes. These dogs are invaluable in a breeding programme and should not be ignored.

In considering the suitability of any stud dog for your bitch remember that you may have to travel with her as the bitch always goes to the dog. Don't be put off by the temptation to just take your bitch to the dog down the road. Every breeder's aim is to breed better stock and this is certainly not the way to do it. A complete outcross (which you would be likely to get if you chose the dog merely for ease of getting to him) would not be likely to put you on the correct path with your breeding programme—far from it, unless the mating proved to be a 'lucky strike'; but you can be assured that the progeny even of this 'lucky strike' would be most unlikely to set you on the road to establishing your own type.

Never use a stud dog without having all details about him; it is wise also to have seen him in the flesh. His temperament should be absolutely irreproachable and sound—this is vitally important. In assessing a stud dog's value to your bitch, particularly if you are line-breeding, you must be able to discriminate between what might be termed hereditary faults and faults brought on by bad rearing, circumstances and environment. Bad feet or coat can easily be caused by the animal having been neglected at an early age. Poor bone structure can be partly due to bad rearing rather than heredity. Faults acquired by bad rearing and environment will not be transmitted but if faults are hereditary they will be passed on to at least some of the dog's progeny. As already stated, a good stud dog should be prepotent and stamp his type on his progeny, but this does not mean that all the pups sired by him will equal his own high quality. Really great prepotent sires, those that have the ability to transmit to their offspring their own characteristics in an exceptional way, are extremely rare in any breed—and here it might be as well to emphasize that any dog that has sired even one puppy showing some inbred fault must carry the gene for that fault in his make-up.

The ideal stud—and that is surely what you are hoping to find for your bitch—should appear a strong, virile animal with a general air of masculinity and a good bold temperament. An effeminate-looking dog can never be classed as a satisfactory stud.

The care of the stud dog is of the greatest importance. He should be kept in a hard condition and never allowed to become over-fat or slack. It is a great mistake to use a stud dog at public stud until he is fully mature. Most breeders will prefer to use a stud dog for the first time on an experienced brood bitch so that the dog is given every chance of an easy mating. The age at which a stud dog is used for the first time depends on the breed as the smaller the breed the earlier he can be used at stud. So much damage can be done by using a dog at stud too early and by over-use he can become sterile at an early age. On the other hand if he is not used for too long it is often difficult to get the dog to understand what is wanted and impossible to get a union. Some breeds are more difficult in this respect than others. A stud dog that does not know his job is a nightmare to handle and so much valuable time can be wasted. If an experienced stud dog is taken to a certain room or part of the garden he will know immediately that he has a visiting bitch and will waste little time in mating her. Mating is covered in detail in the next chapter.

Most owners of stud dogs guard them jealously and take every care to protect them against over use and mis-use and from difficult bitches. It is generally considered unwise to put a dog to regular stud work before the age of about 12 months for the toy breeds and from 18 months to two years for the larger breeds. If used carefully the stud dog should remain quite fertile up to nine or ten years of age. Some stud dogs who have been well looked after throughout their life will continue to sire litters long after ten years but in most cases a dog must be considered to be on the decline at this age. A dog of poor constitution or one that comes from a known strain of bad breeders can never be regarded as a good stud prospect no matter how well he may have been looked after throughout his life.

The best specimens of stud dogs in all breeds are usually available at public stud. It is, therefore, not a wise plan for the novice or the small breeder to keep their own stud dog. If this happens there is a great tendency for the owner to use that dog whether or not he really suits the females' bloodlines and this way no progress can be made with a breeding programme.

Mother Nature has a bad habit of upsetting the apple-cart just when one thinks one is on the right path. However, do not be put off your chosen plan. Do not just breed for today. Breed for the future, and with determination, skill and that little bit of luck you should succeed.

3

Mating & pregnancy

A bitch is usually ready to be mated around about her 10th to 14th day of showing signs of being in season. Just before a bitch starts her season there is a swelling of the vulva and this gradually increases in size before there is any sign of discharge. The discharge usually starts as pale pink, finishing up as blood. The bitch must be watched very carefully at this stage as occasionally the vulva will swell after the first discharge of blood takes place; it is only by watching her behaviour very carefully that you can correctly assess the right day to mate her. This varies from breed to breed and with individual bitches. I have known a bitch to 'take' on her very first day of season and if she is running with a stud dog that you do not want to mate her to, this can be very tiresome. At the other end of the line I have known bitches that will not stand to be mated until their 25th day or even later. All this proves that there is no hard-and-fast day for mating a bitch.

With experience you will soon know when your bitch is ready to be mated; but normally it is when she appears to want to flirt with the other bitches in the kennel. She will twist her tail to one side and even mount them and at this stage her vulva should become rather soft and flabby. If you do not possess any other bitches to test yours with, place your hand very gently across her back just above the root of her tail or across her vulva and if she is ready she will stand rather rigidly and twist her tail from side to side. This is usually a sure indication that she should be mated within the next day or two.

Some breeders use a fertility test to try to make sure that their bitch is ready to be mated. This can be very helpful, particularly if one is sending or taking the bitch any great distance to be mated, as one wants to save time and money by getting the right day and so save a return trip. At the time of ovulation glucose is secreted in the vagina and there is a product on the market which can detect the presence of the glucose. These tapes can be bought from any chemist as they are used for human diabetics. If you think the bitch is ready, insert a small strip of the tape into the vagina and if it turns green within a minute or so then the bitch is ready to be mated 24 hours later. If there is only a small secretion of glucose from the bitch, as there might be in the smaller breeds, only the edges of the tape may change colour.

I have never used this method of testing my bitches and I am sure that you will find with experience it is not a difficult task to mate them on the right day without it and have successful litters.

Many people are under the misapprehension that a bitch will come into season exactly six months from the last time she had her season; they will even count the days and telephone the stud-dog owner to make an appointment for her before she is actually in season. It does not happen this way and although you may make a booking for a particular stud dog in advance (this, of course, is highly necessary), the best procedure to follow then is to inform the stud dog owner immediately you see signs of the bitch's vulva swelling, and a pale pink discharge indicating the first signs of blood.

One stud-dog owner tells the story of a lady telephoning to make an appointment to have her bitch mated on a certain day. On enquiring if this was the correct day the stud-dog owner was told, 'oh yes, it is her birthday and I thought she would like it as a birthday present'. There is never a dull moment in the breeding and showing of dogs!

With toy breeds it is often quite difficult to be certain just when the bitch starts to come into season. Such bitches normally keep themselves very clean and tidy, and the discharge can be negligible. It is quite a good plan to keep toy breeds on a white sheet so that if there is a discharge this can be noticed at the earliest possible time. In the larger breeds the discharge will be much more copious and is not so easily disguised by the bitch.

This external bleeding arises from the breaking down of the walls of the uterus in preparation for the attachment of the fertilized egg, from which will develop the foetus or embryo. During the preliminary period of the oestrum the ovaries discharge the ripe ova or egg cells into the Fallopian tubes and here they remain until they are fertilized, when they pass on into the uterus and attach themselves to the uterine lining, making a placenta. The whelp continues to grow by continuous cell divisions and about the third week each whelp can be felt as a little hard lump. More ova are released than there will be puppies; indeed both ova and sperm are plentiful. If a bitch is mated before ovulation has commenced, i.e. before the discharge of ripe ova from the ovaries, it is likely that only a small litter will result. This also applies if a bitch is mated before ovulation is completed. For this reason a bitch should not be taken to the dog until the coloured discharge has disappeared. Late rather than early matings are to be preferred to ensure that a maximum number of ripe ova is available for fertilization. It has, however, been proved that the sperm cells of the dog can remain active in the reproductive passages of a bitch for about ten days so that ova can be fertilized as they drop into the oviducts by sperms introduced several days before.

Many breeders, particularly with maiden bitches in their own kennels, like to give two services during the bitch's season. Provided a satisfactory mating has taken place and great care has been taken over the timing of the mating I have not found this to be necessary. If these matings are spaced over several days they could lead to complications at the time of whelping as a result of foetuses of different ages being present in the uterus. The number of sperm cells ejected by a normal dog during a mating is very much in excess of the number of ova present.

There is at the present time no known method of controlling the sex of puppies. There are many old wives' tales on this topic but, unfortunately, all have been disproved and we just have to take what we get and be thankful for it. The production of a high proportion of puppies of one sex may be typical of a certain strain or of an individual and could be perpetuated by in-breeding to that individual.

Sometimes bitches have what is commonly known as a false season or pseudo-oestrum. This is very difficult to distinguish from a normal season but if mated the bitch will not prove to be in whelp. She may be quite happy to be mated and show all the normal signs of being in season but some time after the symptoms of heat have disappeared she will come back into season again. In cases of this kind the second heat will be the true period of ovulation and the bitch should be mated again.

Great care must be taken of your bitch when she is in season and if she does get accidentally mated to a wandering minstrel not of your choice the only thing to do is to have her injected to prevent the misalliance being successful. Your Veterinary Surgeon will provide this antidote but on no account can she be mated during the season that will follow. This injection must be given within 24 hours of the mating. The fact that she may have been mated to a mongrel will not affect her future litters from, we hope, your carefully chosen stud dog.

As to the actual mating, this should present very few difficulties provided both animals are normal. The less interference from humans the better. If the stud dog is keen and the bitch brought on the right day a mating should take place very quickly and with a minimum of effort. Both animals should be exercized separately before mating and it is advisable to feed the dogs within a reasonable time after rather than before mating.

As already stated most stud-dog owners prefer to mate a young untried dog to an experienced brood bitch for the first mating as this will give him confidence.

If a visiting bitch is shy and inclined to snap it is far better to tape her as no breeder or stud-dog owner wants to stand the risk of a valuable stud dog being badly bitten, and perhaps put off for ever. Once taped or muzzled the bitch is much easier to control and apart from a little discomfort, there is no harm done. The collar on the bitch should be held tightly at the back of the neck by the left hand whilst the right hand should support her quarters. With a maiden bitch it may be necessary to lubricate the vagina with a little oil or Vaseline. If after several efforts the bitch refuses to co-operate it may well be that she has been presented to the dog too early. Much better to leave her for another day than exhaust the stud dog.

It sometimes happens that maiden bitches have strictures of the vagina and before mating it is wise to pass a well greased clean finger into the vagina. Do this very gently and make sure there is no obstruction. If there is one present this can be very quickly broken down with manipulation and thereafter a mating procured quite happily. In difficult cases consult a Veterinary Surgeon.

A bitch to be mated should never be left to run loose for any length of time with a stud dog. This can be very harmful to the dog and reduce his sexual desires.

When the bitch is absolutely ready to be mated she will draw her tail to one side and stand quietly for the dog while he mounts. Penetration by the dog is usually followed by a 'tie' which by many is considered to be a sign of a successful mating, although it has been proved many times over that a 'tie' is not essential for a successful mating and conception can result without it. Tying can last from just a few moments up to a good half hour and even more, and is caused by the bulbous penis of the dog swelling, and a band of muscles in the bitch's vagina gripping it very tightly so that the pair are locked together, quite unable to come apart until the muscles retract. This is always an indication of a very good mating but it does not necessarily mean that conception will take place.

During the period of the 'tie' the bitch should be held firmly to prevent her becoming restless and perhaps doing some injury to the dog. The dog should be gently helped to bring his front legs down to one side of the bitch and his back leg brought over so that he can stand with his hind-quarters back-to-back with those of the bitch. In this way both parties should be as comfortable as possible and they should remain quiet until natural release takes place. Thereafter the bitch should be removed to her kennel or box, given a drink of water, and allowed to rest. The same procedure applies to the dog but many kennel owners like to sponge the dog's external organs with a mild solution of disinfectant before returning him to his kennel.

The normal period of gestation in a bitch is 63 days. Healthy litters can be born at any time from about the 58th day to the 68th day. Puppies born earlier rarely survive (see whelping chart, page 21).

For the first four or five weeks after mating the bitch should require no change in her routine. If she was not dosed for worms before mating she should be given a vermifuge about two weeks after the completion of her season. The normal practice in my own kennels is that all bitches are wormed as a routine procedure when they come into season and, of course, always at the end of a pregnancy when they leave their puppies.

The in-whelp bitch should be completely free from external parasites and if necessary can be given a bath, although it is absolutely essential that she is dried off completely. A chill contracted at this stage could cause her to abort, or induce metritis, an inflammation of the uterus.

Exercise must be given even up to the last day or two before she whelps. This is essential to keep her in good hard condition and fit her for the job of producing her puppies. As she becomes heavier in whelp her exercising must necessarily be restricted and one must use common sense in this respect. You will find that as she gets more bulky she will cut out her gallops and walk more sedately, as befits her condition. There is the odd bitch, of course, who will still want to have her mad moments but it is better if they can be controlled. The bitch should not be allowed to jump up or down from a height or to squeeze through a narrow door. During the last stages of pregnancy and particularly if she is very heavy in whelp she should not be encouraged to go up and down stairs. Normally the bitch will decide very sensibly for herself what she can and cannot do. The longer a bitch can be persuaded to adhere to her normal routine and take her exercise the better fitted she will be to

GESTATION TABLE

Showing when your bitch is due to whelp

Mated January	Due to whelp March	Mated February	Due to whelp April	Mated March	Due to whelp May	Mated April	Due to whelp June	Mated May	Due to whelp July	Mated June	Due to whelp August	Mated July	Due to whelp September	Mated August	Due to whelp October	Mated September	Due to whelp November	Mated October	Due to whelp December	Mated November	Due to whelp January	Mated December	Due to whelp February
1	5	1	5	1	3	1	3	1	3	1	3	1	2	1	3	1	3	1	3	1	3	1	2
2	6	2	6	2	4	2	4	2	4	2	4	2	3	2	4	2	4	2	4	2	4	2	3
3	7	3	7	3	5	3	5	3	5	3	5	3	4	3	5	3	5	3	5	3	5	3	4
4	8	4	8	4	6	4	6	4	6	4	6	4	5	4	6	4	6	4	6	4	6	4	5
5	9	5	9	5	7	5	7	5	7	5	7	5	6	5	7	5	7	5	7	5	7	5	6
6	10	6	10	6	8	6	8	6	8	6	8	6	7	6	8	6	8	6	8	6	8	6	7
7	11	7	11	7	9	7	9	7	9	7	9	7	8	7	9	7	9	7	9	7	9	7	8
8	12	8	12	8	10	8	10	8	10	8	10	8	9	8	10	8	10	8	10	8	10	8	9
9	13	9	13	9	11	9	11	9	11	9	11	9	10	9	11	9	11	9	11	9	11	9	10
10	14	10	14	10	12	10	12	10	12	10	12	10	11	10	12	10	12	10	12	10	12	10	11
11	15	11	15	11	13	11	13	11	13	11	13	11	12	11	13	11	13	11	13	11	13	11	12
12	16	12	16	12	14	12	14	12	14	12	14	12	13	12	14	12	14	12	14	12	14	12	13
13	17	13	17	13	15	13	15	13	15	13	15	13	14	13	15	13	15	13	15	13	15	13	14
14	18	14	18	14	16	14	16	14	16	14	16	14	15	14	16	14	16	14	16	14	16	14	15
15	19	15	19	15	17	15	17	15	17	15	17	15	16	15	17	15	17	15	17	15	17	15	16
16	20	16	20	16	18	16	18	16	18	16	18	16	17	16	18	16	18	16	18	16	18	16	17
17	21	17	21	17	19	17	19	17	19	17	19	17	18	17	19	17	19	17	19	17	19	17	18
18	22	18	22	18	20	18	20	18	20	18	20	18	19	18	20	18	20	18	20	18	20	18	19
19	23	19	23	19	21	19	21	19	21	19	21	19	20	19	21	19	21	19	21	19	21	19	20
20	24	20	24	20	22	20	22	20	22	20	22	20	21	20	22	20	22	20	22	20	22	20	21
21	25	21	25	21	23	21	23	21	23	21	23	21	22	21	23	21	23	21	23	21	23	21	22
22	26	22	26	22	24	22	24	22	24	22	24	22	23	22	24	22	24	22	24	22	24	22	23
23	27	23	27	23	25	23	25	23	25	23	25	23	24	23	25	23	25	23	25	23	25	23	24
24	28	24	28	24	26	24	26	24	26	24	26	24	25	24	26	24	26	24	26	24	26	24	25
25	29	25	29	25	27	25	27	25	27	25	27	25	26	25	27	25	27	25	27	25	27	25	26
26	30	26	30	26	28	26	28	26	28	26	28	26	27	26	28	26	28	26	28	26	28	26	27
27	31	27	*May* 1	27	29	27	29	27	29	27	29	27	28	27	29	27	29	27	29	27	29	27	28
28	*April* 1	28	2	28	30	28	30	28	30	28	30	28	29	28	30	28	30	28	30	28	30	28	*Mar.* 1
29	2	29	3	29	31	29	*July* 1	29	31	29	31	29	30	29	31	29	31	29	31	29	31	29	2
30	3	—	—	30	*June* 1	30	2	30	*Aug.* 1	30	*Sep.* 1	30	*Oct.* 1	30	*Nov.* 1	30	*Dec.* 1	30	*Jan.* 1	30	*Feb.* 1	30	3
31	4	—	—	31	2	—	—	31	2	—	—	31	2	31	2	—	—	31	2	—	—	31	4

whelp normally and the tougher and hardier her puppies are likely to be.

At the end of the fifth week or so there should be some indications of her condition. A slight thickening of her flanks can be looked for and her teats should show signs of enlarging. At the sixth week it is usually possible for the specialist to detect the presence of foetuses in the uterus. It is not advisable for the amateur to try and detect these foetuses as damage can be done to the bitch.

Sometimes a bitch goes off her food a little during the early weeks of pregnancy but this soon sorts itself out. Other bitches, like humans, suffer from morning sickness which occurs about the third week but here again it soon passes off. Normally bitches eat very well throughout their pregnancy but if a bitch goes off her food altogether round about the sixth or seventh week then it is advisable to seek the help and advice of your Veterinary Surgeon.

After the fourth week it is advisable to step up the diet. If the bitch has been having one large meal a day then it should be increased to two of equal size. It is well to remember that the unborn puppies must be fed via the dam. She must be very well and sensibly nourished. The addition of cod-liver oil, raw eggs and bone meal to the diet can be very beneficial. Milk is a rich natural source of calcium and this mineral is essential for the puppies. The foetuses draw very heavily on the dam for bone formation, and, particularly in the large breeds, if the dam has to supply calcium entirely from her own resources it can cause her to develop eclampsia when she is nursing her litter.

If a bitch is very heavy in whelp it is advisable to increase her meals to three or even four of equal bulk. She will prefer to have her meals rather more often and with less bulk. If there is a big litter there will be a certain amount of pressure on the internal organs and she will find it uncomfortable to eat too much at any one time. This will also tax her digestive system and problems can be avoided with a little thought and careful management.

Fresh water should always be at the bitch's disposal. It is essential that the bitch should not become constipated and if necessary small doses of liquid paraffin should be given. Any aperient that is more violent should be avoided during the pregnancy and particularly at an advanced stage.

Never lift a pregnant bitch by the back of the neck or by the elbows alone. Place one hand under her chest and the other beneath the hind legs so that she is lifted in a horizontal position. Any movement should

A royal visit: Her Majesty the Queen at the
Kennel Club in London on 28 March 1973
— the Centenary Year

Best in Show at Cruft's, 1982

RIGHT
Above` An in-bred pedigree *Below* An outcross pedigree

Westminster Dog Show, the highlight of the American Kennel Club's year, is held in New York every February. *Photo: John L. Ashbey*

Pedigree of ROSSUT STUDENT.

PARENTS	GRAND-PARENTS	G.G.-PARENTS	G.G.G.-PARENTS
SIRE CH. ROSSUT PEANUT. Name / Registration Number / Owner / Address	SIRE ROSSUT CHESTNUT.	SIRE ROSSUT FOREMOST.	SIRE CH. ROSSUT FOREMAN.
			DAM ROSSUT TRUNDLE.
		DAM CH. ROSSUT DAFFODIL.	SIRE ROSSUT GAFFER.
			DAM DIALYNNE &X DEBBIE.
	DAM WEMBURY MORAG OF ROSSUT.	SIRE CH. ROSSUT FOREMAN.	SIRE ROSSUT GAFFER
			DAM CH. ROSSUT COLINBAR PHANTOM.
		DAM TUDORCREST FLEUR OF WEMBURY.	SIRE CH. WEMBURY ARCHIE.
			DAM OUR FLEETWOOD COUNTRY GIRL.
DAM Wembury Morag of Rossut. Name / Registration Number / Owner / Address	SIRE Ch. ROSSUT FOREMAN.	SIRE ROSSUT GAFFER.	SIRE ROSSUT JOKER.
			DAM ROSSUT TRUSTFUL.
		DAM CH. ROSSUT COLINBAR PHANTOM.	SIRE ROSSUT PLUNDER.
			DAM TREETOPS ENVY OF STUBBLESDOWN.
	DAM TUDORCREST FLEUR OF WEMBURY.	SIRE CH. WEMBURY ARCHIE.	SIRE ANNASLINE PAGEMILL PLAYBOY
			DAM WEMBURY TINKERBELL CHANTRESS.
		DAM OUR FLEETWOOD COUNTRY GIRL.	SIRE CH. SOUTHCOURT WEMBURY MERRYBOY.
			DAM FLEETWOOD BEAUTY.

Pedigree of ROSSUT JOKER.

PARENTS	GRAND-PARENTS	G.G.-PARENTS	G.G.G.-PARENTS
SIRE ROZAVEL TEXAS STAR. Name / Registration Number / Owner / Address	SIRE AM. CH. RENOCA'S BEST SHOWMAN.	SIRE AM. CH. OAK HALL SHOWBOAT.	SIRE AM. CH. TRUDY'o TIPTOE.
			DAM AM. CH. SAL-LETO LINDA
		DAM AM. CH. GRA-AN's MORNING JOY.	SIRE AM. CH. C. S GENERAL
			DAM AM. CH. GAYLAD's HEALTHY.
	DAM AM. CH. ROZAVEL RITTER'S MISS BABE.	SIRE AM. CH. JOHNSON'S FANCY KING.	SIRE AM. CH. DUKE SINATRA.
			DAM AM. CH. ROSEHILL MEMORY.
		DAM AM. CH. ROZAVEL RITTERS SWEET SUE.	SIRE INT. CH. THORNRIDGE WRINKLES.
			DAM AM. CH. TAMARACK SWEETCIRCE.
DAM ROSSUT WISTFUL. Name / Registration Number / Owner / Address	SIRE HOLBEIN.	SIRE UNITED PACK BELLMAN	SIRE NORTH BUCKS CHASER.
			DAM NORTH BUCKS BASHFUL.
		DAM ETON COLLEGE VIPER.	SIRE OLD BERKELY LOCKSMITH.
			DAM ETON COLLEGE VIGILANT.
	DAM VERONESE.	SIRE AMPLEFORTH PLUNDER.	SIRE WARWICKSHIRE PROMISE.
			DAM AMPLEFORTH DEWDROP.
		DAM ETON COLLEGE VIPER.	SIRE OLD BERKELY LOCKSMITH.
			DAM ETON COLLEGE VIGILANT.

Visiting bitches that are aggressive or difficult to mate should be muzzled or taped to avoid injury to the stud dog or those in attendance

It should be every breeder's aim to breed
to type: here is a Golden Retriever's litter
all very even and typical

A whelping box, with a rail round it to
protect the whelps

A very placid dam giving her puppies one
of their last drinks of mother's milk

A very promising Beagle dog puppy at
eight weeks, with strong head, bone and
substance; he has already been taught to
stand on a table

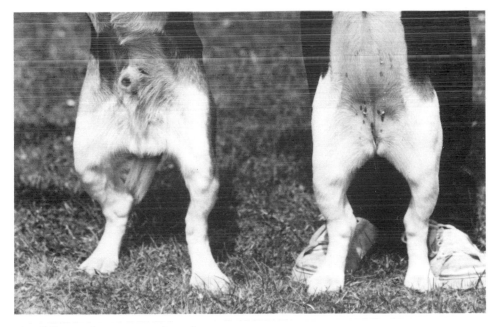

The difference between a male and a
female; the male is on the left

The correct way to hold a very young
puppy

be done very gently and carefully and at all costs sudden jerking movements should be avoided.

A bitch can show all the symptoms of being in whelp but when the due date arrives fail to produce any puppies. This phenomenon is known as a false pregnancy; it is very disappointing for everybody and the poor bitch can become very distressed. She has made her bed all ready for her whelps, then nothing turns up and she just does not understand why she has no puppies. To calm her down and comfort her it is a very good idea to give her one of her special toys or an old towel—anything that she can cuddle and pretend is a puppy. Bitches soon get over this unhappy state but regrettably there is no satisfactory answer to the problem. The bitch increases in girth up to about the sixth or seventh week and in many cases even produces milk all ready for her whelps. False pregnancy can also occur in an unmated bitch, more particularly in a rather nervous and highly strung one. In such cases the bitch should be freely exercised, fed rather scantily and given an aperient. Her water intake should be cut down to a very minimum. It is generally thought advisable to mate bitches that are susceptible to false pregnancies on their next season.

4

Whelping & the nursing mother

Having watched your bitch advance in her pregnancy, you will want to be prepared for her actual whelping and have everything at hand for the big moment.

A litter may consist of anything from one to 15 or 16 puppies depending on the breed. Litters of one are, unfortunately, quite common in the toy breeds; litters of 15 and 16, although recorded, are much more rare. The number in a litter is not everything. I am always much happier to have a good, even, moderate-sized litter of puppies than to have an exceptionally large litter of puppies varying in size and strength. In a larger litter, unless one resorts to bottle rearing, the weaklings usually die anyway, and I am sure that Mother Nature never really intended that they should live. The motto of all good breeders should surely be: quality and type before quantity and indifferent specimens.

The bitch should be introduced to her whelping-box about ten days before her due date. The box, made of wood, must be large enough for her to turn round in comfortably and about 2in (5cm) from the floor; there should be a rail round the box. This allows the puppies to be protected when the bitch lies down or turns round and can save a whelp or two from being crushed by the bitch. This can so easily happen if the litter is a big one—no matter how careful the mother is accidents can happen and it is best to try to prevent this. My ideal whelping-box has a lid on top that lifts up, enabling an infra-red lamp to hang over the bitch and family if required. The box has a wire-fronted front door that can be kept closed if necessary. Beneath this door there is a further strip of solid wood that can be folded down when the puppies are ready to come out of the box but until they are old enough this strip of wood, which is on hinges, is held in an upright position by two bolts at either side of the box. Underneath the box is enough room for a heater to be put into position.

24

Most breeders find newspapers the best material for whelping a bitch on. Her natural reaction as she draws close to her due date is to get into her box, tear the newspaper into shreds and distribute it around her box to her own satisfaction. She may repeat this for several days before she actually settles down to whelp. A new type of bedding is now on the market (known in Britain as Vet-Bed), and this is proving very successful as a floor-covering for the whelping bed. It can be bought to fit the bed—if you have two or three bits the whelping bed can be kept clean and hygienic. The material absorbs a great deal of the liquid that is present in any whelping and helps to keep the bed dry, although the underfloor heating is also a great help in this respect. The bitch's whelping quarters should be kept scrupulously clean at all times. She must be kept warm and comfortable as heat to the nursing mother and her whelps is of the very greatest importance. This cannot be stressed too much, as many whelps die, particularly in the early stages, because of cold. The temperature for whelping should not fall below 70°F (21°C) and this should be maintained for about the first week. Thereafter it can be eased down very gradually.

Artificial heat can be supplied in various ways but at all times the dogs must be protected from it. Paraffin (kerosene) stoves should never be used because of the tremendous risk of fire. Any heat source should ideally be at ground level, since heat rises. This unfortunately is not always either practical or safe because unless it is guarded in some way the dogs will have access to it with disastrous results. Electrical tubular heaters placed under the whelping bed are an ideal way of providing the necessary heat, as experience has shown, but one must make very sure that if the puppies fall out of bed they cannot get under the bed to the heater. I learned this lesson from experience as unfortunately I once discovered two puppies from a litter fast asleep under the bed and they had very bad burn marks on their heads. These burn marks did not deter them from remaining near the heater but they had nasty scars even after the burns had healed. This naturally spoilt their appearance when they came to be sold on to their new homes and it had to be rather special people that took these 'marked' babies. Having learned my lesson I now always very carefully put bricks round the entire whelping box leaving no hole through which the youngsters can creep through to the heater.

I also use infra red lamps above the whelping box. These should be carefully checked before use and the flex should never be within easy access of the dog. There are two types of infra red lamps, the bright emitter and the dull emitter. They should be suspended at a height of not less than 18in (45cm) above the bed. They are used extensively in whelping quarters and provided they are used sensibly can be invaluable. In our own kennels when the time comes to give less heat to the bitch and her puppies we take away the top heater and put the lid down on her box. We find that if the top heater is kept on too long over the puppies it tends to dry their skin up a little too much. We prefer to leave the underfloor heater on and pack the bitch out with wood-wool. In this way we have reared very many successful litters.

To help you prepare for the whelping, here is a checklist of things you should not be without—they should be available close at hand. At a crucial moment, it is no good having to leave the bitch, because of your own lack of preparedness, to go to another part of the house for, say, a pair of scissors or a towel. There is enough to think about when a whelping starts, and a small problem of this kind could lead to the loss of one of the whelps.

Whelping room equipment

Sack (for disposal of newspapers and towels)
Cotton wool
Good antiseptic
Vaseline
Rough towel (for drying the whelps)
Nail brush, soap, and bowl of hot water (for washing hands)
Kitchen scales and notebook (for recording details of whelps)
Animal thermometer
Clock or watch (for recording intervals between whelps)
Kitchen paper (for mopping up)
Ballpoint pen or pencil
Surgical scissors already sterilized
Tweezers
Sturdy table (in case of examination of bitch by Veterinary Surgeon)
Good lighting, and torch (flashlight) in case of emergency
Packet of glucose
Milk drink for bitch
Water bowl and supply of fresh water (for bitch)
Cardboard box lined with towel, and with hot-water bottle (in case puppies have to be moved for a period of time, if only so you can clean the bitch's bed)

It may also be useful to have at hand some brandy; this is for the bitch or the whelps, and not for those assisting—although you may well feel like a drop afterwards, particularly if it has been a difficult whelping!

Having got your bitch safely installed in her warm, comfortable whelping quarters, you now settle down to watch for the first signs of labour. If you take the bitch's temperature at this stage it should have fallen to about 2°F below normal (normal temperature is 101.5°F (38.5°C)). You should see the bitch strain, gently to begin with, and then with more drive. When this becomes more frequent and increases in intensity a water bag should appear. Keep a close eye on the bitch at this stage but try to do so unobtrusively and do not interfere, unless you think there is a problem. Bitches, even maiden bitches (that is, bitches having their first litter), are quite marvellous on their own and manage so well that any outside interference, from you, is not welcome nor appreciated. The mother is well able to get on with the job and if you insist on interfering you will probably find that she will give up doing her job and let you get on with it. This is not a very satisfactory state of affairs and you will only be making a rod for your own back.

If you do feel that things are not going quite right, do get help from your Veterinary Surgeon, unless you have had plenty of experience. In fact it is a good idea to let him know that you have a bitch due to whelp: if he has been warned, and you have to hook him out in the middle of the night, he will not feel quite so bad about it! If you are worried don't wait until the morning—it could be too late to save a whelp or even your bitch. No conscientious Veterinary Surgeon will ever object to coming to your aid if you warn him beforehand.

The water bag is not to be mistaken for a puppy. A puppy will be hard and solid to the touch because the head of the whelp should appear first. The water bag will be quite soft to the touch and its shape will be governed by the length of time it has been visible. After the water bag has burst the bitch will make further great efforts to strain and push and so finally expel the first whelp. The head of the puppy should be followed by the fore-limbs and the remainder of the body will follow quite easily. The puppy may arrive completely contained in the sac or this may have been already broken in the process of the birth. The whelp is attached to the umbilical cord and this is attached at the other end to the placenta. The placenta is generally expelled from the bitch either with the puppy or very soon after the puppy is born. It is a spongy organ which has nourished the puppy during its growth in the uterus. The sac is ruptured by the bitch and then she proceeds to bite through the umbilical cord and to swallow the placenta, or 'after-birth'. It is absolutely essential that the bitch gets rid of each after-birth as if it is retained in the uterus it can cause serious trouble, such as metritis. Most bitches instinctively eat the after-births: I have always felt that if nature intends that the bitch should do this it is better for her to carry on rather than have her upset by taking it away from her.

If you have reason to think that the bitch is not getting rid of the after-births and retaining them, get in touch with your Veterinary Surgeon who will give the bitch an injection of pituitrin to help expel them from the uterus.

If the bitch expels the puppy in the bag and seems rather un-interested or does not seem to know what to do, act quickly by opening the sac just above the whelp's head, and pull the bag off thus allowing the newborn to breathe. If the action is delayed the puppy can drown in the sac or at the very least take quite a time to revive. If the bitch is happy for you to help her, dry off her puppies as they are born. There is no harm in doing this and it does save her quite a lot of exertion particularly if the litter is a large one. Have a clean rough towel available, and holding the whelp very firmly use the towel to give it a good rough dry. Do not be afraid that you will damage the puppy—puppies are very tough and can take a lot of rough rubbing to bring them to life. In drying them off well you will get their circulation going and thereafter they can be given back to their dam all ready to grab one of her teats and contentedly feed from it. Do not give up easily with a whelp that seems unwilling to respond. If it appears rather lifeless keep rubbing it well with the towel; if it seems to have quite a bit of mucus or fluid in its air passages, hold it very carefully in the towel with its head uppermost and well supported, lift it above your head, and bring it down as sharply as possible as you would do to bring down the mercury in a thermometer. Repeat this performance several times and it will help remove the liquid from the puppy. It will also help bring life to the puppy. If you hear even a slight whimper you will know that you are succeeding and that the puppy is beginning to come to, and you must continue with the exercise until the whelp seems quite lively. It can then be returned to its mother and if she starts to lick it and push it in to her teats all should be well.

Another method of resuscitation is to put the whelp up to its neck in a bucket of cold water and then, briefly, into very hot water. For this method you must make very sure that the whelp, which becomes rather slippy and slimy to touch, does not get out of your grasp and fall into either the hot or the cold water.

Yet another method is mouth-to-mouth resuscitation. Unless you have had experience of this, you are not likely to be successful, as in blowing air into the lungs it so often happens that at the same time you blow air into the stomach. This is detrimental to the puppy: air in its stomach will prevent it from breathing properly. It should be realized that a whelp cannot begin to breathe properly until the brain is properly oxygenated—only when this happens can respiration or circulation take place at all.

If the birth is normal most bitches will continue to lick their new-born babies very thoroughly and thereafter push them in to their teats to be nourished. With a maiden bitch it is advisable just to keep an eye on her and see that she performs her task correctly and happily. There is nothing more satisfying than to watch a good brood deliver her puppies, and when she is finished to have them all beautifully clean and tidy and lined up at the teats. She looks proud of them and so she should be: this is always a very exciting and proud moment for the breeder, who will want to take the first opportunity to check the whelps to see what colour and sex they are.

If the bitch does require assistance with the severing of the umbilical cord, and this is sometimes the case with the very short-nosed breeds such as Pekingese, Bostons, Pugs, French Bulldogs, etc., then cut the cord with sterilized scissors about one inch from the stomach. The umbilical cord should need no further attention and it will dry off and disappear altogether in a few days.

If perchance your bitch is unfortunate enough to have a breech birth, which is caused by the puppy's being wrongly presented at the entrance to the pelvis, she may need a little help from you. Such an abnormality in presentation is one of the most common causes of whelping problems in a bitch. As already described the normal position for a foetus in the pelvis is with the head directed outwards. If a puppy is reversed so that the back end, i.e. the tail and hind-legs, comes first, although this is not normal, it does not usually present any difficulties. It is, however, advisable in such cases to help the puppy gently along by easing and very carefully and gently pulling the hind-legs as the dam strains. If the birth is delayed the puppy may suffocate. If the puppy lies across the womb it can be very difficult to manipulate and should be attended to by a Veterinary Surgeon. A very skilful manipulator may just be able to turn the whelp into the correct position for presentation, but please leave this to those experienced enough to try. Unfortunately, if it is not possible to move a whelp that is presented across the womb, your Veterinary Surgeon may have to use forceps, or if that is not possible, resort to a Caesarian Section.

If the puppy is presented normally but the head is misplaced either by being pressed against the chest with the nose pointing downwards or by being forced upwards for some reason, live delivery could be very difficult. Here again your Veterinary Surgeon should be called but if professional assistance is not immediately available in such an emergency, and to avoid exhausting your bitch, you should go to her help and try to draw the head into the correct position. Never ever use forceps yourself as you will probably do more damage than good. Very carefully scrub your hands so that there is no likelihood of passing on any infection. Lubricate your fingers with oil or Vaseline, very gently insert your first two fingers into the bitch and press the puppy back until it is clear of the opening of the womb. Always remember never to use any force in case you injure any part of the very tender reproductive organs of the bitch. You must also be careful not to press the puppy backwards when the bitch is trying to push it forward. You should press only in the intervals between the bitch's straining. When the whelp has been pushed back the head should then be lifted up or pushed down, according to the problem; when the bitch strains again the head should come forward correctly, and you can gently guide the body downwards to achieve a successful birth.

Even if you are nervous do try to be very placid about the whole exercise. If you panic at all it will only upset her when she is doing her best to expel her puppies. Keep calm, talk gently to her and reassure her that she is doing well and that everything is under control. If you can help her in this way and produce live puppies from a difficult whelping you will have done a very good job and gained valuable experience.

Another complication in whelping does arise on occasions, when everything looks normal and the head arrives first but there is difficulty in getting the body expelled. This could be due to a particularly large puppy and unfortunately these large puppies very often come first. The membranes should be broken at the mouth of the puppy to enable the whelp to breathe a little in spite of the fact that its lungs are still restricted. Try to hold the whelp at the top of its neck just below its head. Do this with your first two fingers, or your finger and thumb if you can get them through. Ladies' hands are much more useful for this exercise as men usually find that their hands are not slim enough to get through. Once you get a grip, hold on steadily until the bitch strains, then pull the head downwards and forwards and hope that the whelp comes away. If it does not, wait until the bitch strains again and do the same exercise, but on this occasion pull the head gently to one side and then to the other in the hope that this will release the shoulders. If there is a limb or foot protruding, pull that leg forward and outwards towards the bitch's tail. This should release one shoulder and the same should then be done with the other. A slight corkscrew action will very often help to deliver a whelp that is reluctant to come away and is tightly wedged. It is always such a relief when, after struggling with a difficult whelping, you bring the puppy away in your hand. Waste no time in getting the cord severed and getting the whelp dried off. If the bitch is not distressed by your doing this, all to the good: it will give her a little time to relax and recover from the pain and discomfort that she is obviously having to endure.

It is difficult to estimate exactly how long any whelping will last. It depends on too many things: the size of the litter, the breed, whether it is a first litter or an experienced brood bitch and so on.

Some bitches manage to produce four or five puppies in quick succession whilst others can take four or five hours. It is all a very natural happening. Some dams accept it naturally and are marvellous broods whilst others make a fuss about it, or don't exert themselves very much. This sort will let you do as much of the dirty work as possible and would have you even clean the whelps if you were so disposed. Like some human beings, some bitches are natural mothers, and others are certainly not. Most bitches do appreciate being given a hot drink in between each whelp. Their tongues get very parched with all the work they have to do in licking their babies and cleaning up. Some hot milk is usually very acceptable but if not try some water and glucose.

In between the arrivals of the whelps the paper in the bed will get very mucky and sodden. Try to remove and replace as much of this as possible (see page 25) so that the bitch and her puppies are comfortable.

Once your bitch has finished whelping she should be taken outside to relieve herself. This gives you or your assistant an opportunity to clean the bed and check on the whelps for sex, colour and weight. Many breeders like to weigh their puppies at birth so that an accurate account can be kept of their progress. This is an extremely good plan and I keep a special book just to register the progress of litters and to report on any particular points in respect of the actual whelping that might be of use to us in a future whelping by that bitch.

When the bitch is taken outside the handler must watch her

behaviour—whether or not she seems settled and whether she seems constipated or inclined to be rather loose in her motions. The bitch will be anxious to get back to her new family and may not feel inclined to waste any time even to relieve herself. Don't be cross if she does this indoors just when you have settled her down and gone to get a little refreshment yourself. Maiden bitches are particularly anxious about their new family but will soon settle with sensible treatment.

It is often difficult to know whether or not a bitch has actually finished whelping and this is particularly so with a large litter. A retained whelp is a great source of infection particularly if it has been dead for some time and the longer it is left there the more ill the bitch will become, not only will she suffer, but also her whelps. If she seems unsettled do take her temperature and if this is high call your Veterinary Surgeon straight away. In our own kennels we make a habit of giving an injection of pituitrin when we are reasonably certain that the bitch has finished whelping. This expels any retained placenta or whelp that may have been harbouring in the uterus. If a dead puppy or placenta is present its presence will be indicated by a thick dark green nasty discharge which can be very offensive. If this is seen you must contact your Veterinary Surgeon straight away in the hope that he can save the life of your bitch. This is a very serious situation and there must be no delay in getting the help of your vet.

Whelping can be delayed through the complete absence of any labour contractions or by their being too ineffective and infrequent to produce the puppies. This problem is known as uterine inertia and here again pituitrin can come to the rescue and your Veterinary Surgeon will inject the quantity required for your breed of bitch. As a stimulant pituitrin is usually most effective but if this fails it may be necessary to resort to surgical help. It does not necessarily follow that if a bitch has had one Caesarian she will have to have one the next time. Generally I give her another chance but if complications arise next time I reckon that particular bitch to be as a bad breeding prospect, and do not breed from her again. The problem could be a hereditary trait, and she might very well pass it on to her female progeny.

In very rare circumstances a bitch will deliberately eat or kill her whelps. This usually happens with an over-excitable bitch which, when trimming the umbilical cord, accidentally nips it off too near the stomach and in doing so tears the wall of the stomach. In trying to make matters better she keeps on licking the stomach until she has made quite a hole in it and in her desperation to sort out this mess she kills the whelp. When she realizes it is dead she often eats the whelp just as she would do an after-birth. Such excitable bitches should be watched very carefully; if they show any sign of negligence in this respect it is better to take the puppies away from them and sever the umbilical cord oneself. The bitch can be given the whelp back once it has been dried and provided she accepts it, cuddles it, gently licks it all over and pushes it towards a teat, she should be trusted with any further whelps once you have cleaned and dried them for her. A bitch that attempts to eat her pups in her first litter can prove to be a very good mother in a later litter and it is worthwhile giving her the chance to rear her litter herself. She is not vicious, but just over-anxious and rather excited about the whole new experience of whelping and looking after her new family.

In breeds that might tend to attempt to eat their offspring, such as some of the Terrier breeds, breeders usually release the whelp from its foetal envelope, attend to the umbilical cord, and having dried the puppy put it in a small heated box with its other brothers and sisters until the bitch has finished. Then and only then are they presented to her and if this is done very carefully she will accept them, lick them, and proceed to care for them very well.

For 24 hours after whelping feed the bitch only with liquid nourishment or a very thin gruel. Bitches will often be rather loose in their bowel movements. This is quite normal but after a few days there should be a return to normal. If diarrhoea persists something must be done to counteract it, as it will affect the bitch's health very quickly; with a litter to rear she can do without any further complications. Seek the help of your Veterinary Surgeon, as the cause of diarrhoea can be difficult to determine. The same applies if the bitch is constipated. A dose of castor oil or some other good laxative will usually do the trick but if not seek professional help. For the first few days a bitch may be disinclined to leave her whelping room but it is essential that she be given the opportunity three or four times a day to empty her bladder and bowels. She will feel much more comfortable and settled if she gets into the habit of doing this and it will be for the good of her family and herself.

Puppies that are born earlier than the 57th day of gestation stand little chance of survival. Premature puppies need very careful nursing and they must be kept in a very warm temperature, i.e. 70°F (21°C). At first they may not be able to suck perhaps because of a lack of strength or because the bitch's teats are too big for their tiny mouths. In such cases they must be bottle-fed until they are strong enough to take from their dam. Premature labour is not very common in bitches and is usually brought on as a result of an accident, a shock or some severe illness.

The following mixture for bottle feeding puppies is a very simple one and one that we have had great success with. Mix 1 tsp. of glucose with the yolk of an egg and add this to ½ pint of hot milk. There are also several ready-prepared puppy milk foods on the market, although breeders usually have their own recipe that has proved successful for them. Good small baby-feeding bottles can be bought from any good chemist and these are ideal for the job. If the whelps are very tiny (and especially for the toy breeds) it might be better initially to use a premature-baby feeding bottle with a very small teat. Any bottle must be sterilized before use and to ensure that it is perfectly clean a small brush designed for this purpose should be used. Always ensure that the temperature of the milk is right for the whelps. To test this drop a few spots on the back of your hand; if this is comfortable to the touch the milk will be the right temperature for the puppies.

The nursing mother must be carefully looked after and at all times protected from any undue disturbances. She must be kept warm and comfortable as heat is so important both to the mother and her babies. Many whelps die in the early stages because of lack of it.

The first milk that the bitch produces after parturition is known as colostrum and this is very rich in vitamins A and D. It is from colostrum that the puppies get their first supply of antibodies which protect them from the many bacteria that they will encounter in their new world. It also acts as a purgative and clears the puppies' intestines of any faeces which might have accumulated in the bowel up to birth. Puppies deprived of this first milk are at a great disadvantage and are much more susceptible to infections that other puppies are better able to fight. This first milk is vitally important and all whelps should have their share of it if at all possible.

The nursing mother should be examined every day for any sore spots, abrasions or swellings. This particularly applies to her teats. They should be kept immaculately clean and watched most carefully for any signs of cracks or soreness. In a normal healthy litter the whelps will find their own way to their milk supply in the nipples and if they seem a little backward at coming forward a good mother will nudge them on to a teat. If a pup does not seem to manage to grasp a teat by itself its mouth can be very gently opened and the nipple inserted. This will usually give it the idea and it should be quite quick to understand that if it sucks it will be provided with nourishment. If not, squeeze a little milk into its mouth very carefully from the base of the nipple. The dam may be slightly upset at this unnatural interference but usually she accepts your help and looks pleased when all the whelps settle down to their job; she will usually carry on from there looking after her new family. The bitch's milk glands must be watched very carefully in case there is an excess of milk which will cause her great pain and discomfort if not attended to immediately. In such a case massage the breasts with a little warm oil before attempting to draw any milk off. Inverted or indrawn teats can be drawn out by careful manipulation with the fingers.

As the pups grow older they make more demands on the dam's teats and sore, cracked nipples often appear. Do watch this very carefully as apart from the continual tugging at the teats by the healthy pups whose milk teeth will also be coming through there is the problem of sharp little claws. Puppies' nails grow at an astonishing rate and when puppies are about ten days old their nails must be trimmed. Thereafter this should be done about once a week until the puppy is old enough for it not to be necessary. When the puppy is still in the whelping quarters it is quite easy to avoid the quick as it is very obvious at this stage and looks pink in appearance. The cutting of nails should preferably be done with proper nail-clippers and not with nail-scissors. When the puppy is old enough to take exercise on a hard surface toe-nails will require very little further attention.

As the puppies grow older the bitch's teats become even more vulnerable and as the puppies go through the usual rhythmic motions with their little feet on the dam's breasts abrasions do appear. To avoid any suffering to the bitch treat any abrasions immediately. They should be bathed gently, dried very carefully and dusted with boracic powder. If necessary a healing salve should be used. Cutting the puppies' claws regularly will help prevent further damage to the bitch.

If the litter is small, some of the teats can be neglected as the whelps will always go to the teats offering the best supply of milk. Who can blame them? This can cause milk to congeal in the unused mammae which will become very hard, inflamed and sore. This must be attended to immediately as it can cause the dam great pain and discomfort; in extreme cases she will refuse to feed her whelps and go off her food. Here again the affected parts should be bathed in warm water, massaged with oil and when soft have the milk drained from them. If this has happened once, great care must be taken not to allow it to

35

happen again and a careful watch must be kept on these teats to make sure that the puppies are not deserting them and just drawing off the milk from a few nipples.

Dew claws are to be found on the inner side of each fore-foot, corresponding with the human thumb in position. Sometimes they appear on the hind-feet but are seldom attached there by more than skin and are very easily removed. Dew claws should be amputated from the front legs a few days after birth. They should be cut off close to the limb with a pair of rounded surgical scissors that have been sterilized. Any bleeding that may occur can be quickly and effectively arrested by dabbing the wound with permanganate of potash. If this very small operation is left to a later stage, as it sometimes has to be perhaps because of inexperience on the part of the breeder, when blood and nerve supplies to the dew claws are fully developed, it is much wiser to have the operation done under local anaesthesia by a Veterinary Surgeon.

I feel that all show dogs should have their dew claws removed; their removal gives the legs a very much cleaner look, but also dew claws can so often be a source of worry to the dog if they get caught in undergrowth whilst they are out exercising. This can cause a very nasty tear that causes the dog pain and discomfort and often these tears take a long time to heal. With the smaller breeds of dogs, which one is inclined to lift up to have a word with, the dew claws can catch in knitted jerseys or pullovers or even just in stockings. The claws become badly torn and give the dog unnecessary suffering apart altogether from any damage that can be done to clothes etc. If the dew claws are taken off about three days after birth they will cause no further trouble to the dog or anyone else.

Very rarely are dew claws mentioned in the official breed standards, so one can only presume that as they serve no useful purpose the dog is better without them. One standard that does mention hind dew claws is that of the Pyrenean Mountain Dog which specifically states that the hind-legs should each carry strongly made double dew claws and the lack of them is a serious breed fault. No mention is made of front dew claws.

If a dew claw does become broken the break is nearly always through the quick. In this case it is necessary to cut the broken piece off as soon as possible with one quick sharp snip of the clippers. Any bleeding can be stopped very quickly by applying cotton wool and a bandage.

The docking of the tail in breeds that require it according to the official standard is at the moment rather a controversial subject. Some Veterinary Surgeons approve of it and some do not. The reasons are many but having docked very many litters in my life I have never yet lost a puppy and I have to be persuaded that there is any real suffering involved in docking. Most established breeders dock their own puppies' tails at 3–4 days old. In fact they prefer to do it themselves as they know exactly how much to take off the tail and how much to leave on. The tail must be docked at the right spot to give the correct outline to the dog and if for the particular breed the dog should be left with two-thirds of its tail it can look quite unbalanced if left with only one-third, which would spoil that particular dog's chances in the show ring. While the docking is taking place the dam should be taken out for a walk out of earshot of any squeaks that her puppies may make.

For docking the tail should be held just about the point where it is to be severed. The skin should be drawn well back towards the body and then the scissors can cut through the cartilage and the skin will move forward again and cover the cut surface. If it is done properly little or no bleeding will occur but if there does happen to be a tendency to bleed the wound can be dabbed with permanganate of potash. When the dam returns to her puppies she will lick them and so help heal the wound; but at this stage all her whelps truly think of is getting back onto her teats; and in a few seconds they will be contentedly sucking. In years to come it may be that docking will be banned and we will have a new line in undocked Boxers, Dobermanns, Poodles, Cockers, Rottweilers and many others like them.

Eclampsia can occur in the nursing mother at any time whilst she is nursing her litter but it is more likely to happen during the later stages of nursing. This condition is caused by a lack of calcium in the bloodstream. Her own supply of calcium is excreted, via her milk, to her puppies and a good mother will give everything that she has got to give to her puppies and completely drain herself. A very heavy demand is made at this time upon her own resources in order to produce a correct supply of calcium in her milk for her babies. It is essential that the calcium is replenished by giving her a supply in her own food.

The symptoms of eclampsia are very easy to recognize. The bitch becomes very weak and finds difficulty in even standing up. She has a far away look in her eyes and begins to lose interest in everything including her whelps. If this condition is allowed to persist she may even have convulsions when she will lie on her side and foam at the mouth. This is very worrying and distressing to watch and it is imperative that you contact your Veterinary Surgeon straightaway as time is very important. A large dose of calcium should be injected subcutaneously by the vet as without this aid the bitch will surely die quite quickly. The cure is quite certain if the mother is treated in time but I cannot impress upon you enough that speed is of the utmost importance.

To safeguard your bitch against eclampsia you must feed her well. The amount, of course, depends on the size of the bitch and the number of whelps. Using your own discretion and knowing how you fed the bitch before she was mated, feed only light food, such as chicken or fish for the first three days; then give four meals per day. Her four meals should consist of raw meat with a little biscuit meal added plus a good allowance of milk. Fresh water should always be available to the bitch. If it is a winter litter I would suggest that you add cod-liver oil to her food. For summer litters this can sometimes overheat the bitch's bloodstream making her hot and uncomfortable. Both summer and winter I add ordinary animal bone meal: this supplies the extra calcium that is necessary at this time. It helps produce good bone substance in the breeds where it is required—most, with the exception of the toy breeds. It also prevents rickets in the big breeds, and helps to avert the problem of eclampsia already described.

A good strong brood bitch in most breeds will happily rear five or six puppies without any trouble at all. If she is left with nine or ten whelps it is advisable to help her by supplementary bottle feeding of the whelps. A toy bitch should not be expected to rear more than four healthy puppies without help. If large litters are reared it is likely that several of the whelps will suffer if they do not get supplementary food and they will grow up to be weaklings, not truly representative of the breed concerned. The bitch will also suffer and take far too much out of herself. It is surely much more satisfactory to rear five or six good puppies than ten of inferior quality.

A foster mother can be most useful to help in the rearing of a large family or when a bitch is unable to feed and rear her puppies. Breeders who know that a bitch is unlikely to rear a litter satisfactorily will make arrangements to mate another bitch, even a cross-bred or mongrel, at the same time so that she can help out with the rearing of the puppies. This is particularly so when the breeder is very anxious to hold on to a bitch's bloodline. Valuable puppies are worth saving and bottle rearing is never the same as a good foster mother if you can get one. The work of bottle rearing is continuous and endless and often, after great patience, quite fruitless.

The puppies should be taken from the dam with a minimum of fuss and as unobtrusively as possible. They should be smeared with some milk from the foster mother and gently slipped into her bed. Once she licks them and nuzzles them against her it can be safely assumed that she will look after them. The foster's puppies should be withdrawn from her and taken quickly out of sight and hearing of their mother. If the original dam is distraught because of the loss of her own whelps one or two of the foster's puppies can be given to her. The earlier after a foster's whelping the transfer can be done the easier it will be. The rest of the litter should be destroyed immediately by euthanasia. This must be done humanely. In my kennels we have a device supplied by the RSPCA, a metal box into the bottom compartment of which the whelps are put. Above this compartment there is an inner lid with a small meshed hole, and here one puts cotton wool that has been soaked in chloroform. Then the strong outer lid is fastened down firmly, excluding any air from the whelps inside. Through a window in the front of the box the whelps can be observed as they go to sleep, very peacefully with no struggling or pain. If you do not have such a facility, you should take the whelps to your Veterinary Surgeon who will give them an injection.

If a foster is brought in to nurse the whelps make sure that she is in every way healthy and free from any parasites. The temperament of the foster mother is very important as she will play a great part in the upbringing of your puppies, and there is no doubt that environment can affect a puppy's temperament.

Cats can make very good fosters for the toy breeds and can rear three or four toy puppies with ease and loving care. They are most gentle and can make wonderful mothers. So many cats are unwanted when their owners find that they have produced a litter of kittens. They are put in a box by their owners and rushed off to the nearest Veterinary Surgeon for destruction. Quite often one can rescue such a cat from an Animal Hospital; in return you will be handsomely rewarded by an excellent foster to rear your litter of puppies. Thereafter she will surely deserve a permanent home with you.

If for any reason your bitch has to have medication make sure that the instructions of your Veterinary Surgeon are carried out to the full. Do not think that because she seems all right again that it is not necessary to finish a course of antibiotics prescribed. To give only half the course or even just miss the last day is courting disaster as this will breed a race of bacteria that will be tolerant of the medication.

Always check the bitch over for fleas or other parasites. When she goes out to the garden she may easily pick up some of these trouble-makers and the sooner you spot them the better. They must be picked out of her coat by hand; at this stage you must not spray the bitch as the young whelps could easily lick her with bad results.

Check her teats each day and if she has got them dirty from being out in the garden gently wash and dry them. Her hindquarters should be washed at least once a day particularly if she is a long-coated breed. She should be made as clean and fresh as possible and she will appreciate all your efforts. The discharge from her vulva will stick to her coat and make her uncomfortable and this should be washed and gently combed out. It should clear up in a day or two and if it does not veterinary advice should be sought. The initial discharge is followed by a blood discharge which comes from the wall of the uterus where the placentas were attached. After three or four weeks this begins to clear and the uterus will return to its near-normal size.

Some bitches begin to get a bit tired of their puppies continually chasing after them and at about five weeks after whelping I find it a good idea to give the bitch a low table to jump on to where she can sit and watch her puppies, but where they cannot get to her. It is surprising how the mothers like to use this escape-route and with the knowledge that they can get away from their puppies if they want to, they seem to take more interest in keeping them clean and feeding them.

Start to take the nursing mother away from her whelps from about five weeks onwards depending, of course on the size of the litter. If she has only one puppy or two at the most she hardly needs to be weaned from them at all and this will just happen automatically. This is particularly true of the smaller breeds.

It is best to start taking the bitch away from her puppies during the day and for a short period to begin with, increasing each day until by seven weeks she is away most of the day and just going back at night. At this stage one must check on her teats so make sure that they are not hard and uncomfortable and if so they must be massaged and bathed as described on page 35.

Between seven and eight weeks, take her away at night and if she is loaded with milk in the morning let her puppies suck from her for just a few minutes first thing in the morning. Do this for a morning or two and you should find that her milk glands will sort themselves out. If she still seems to have quite a lot of milk take her away from her puppies altogether, night and day, and give her a good dose of epsom salts, the dose being according to the size of the bitch. For beagle size give 1 tablespoonful and so on up and down the line. The bitch won't like this exercise and if she will not take it on her food it is best to pop it down her throat and then hold her mouth shut until it is all gone. During this operation water should be kept away from her, only a sip morning and night being allowed. Two days of the epsom salt treatment is usually enough to stop her milk. Keep her on a lean diet during this period.

Once finished and dried off from her puppies it is well to worm her. She will certainly have worms and the sooner you can get rid of them the better. After all this she should be bathed and groomed and, if necessary, trimmed so that she is ready to lead a normal life. She may have lost quite a bit of coat during her motherhood but with care and attention this will soon grow again. If she is a show bitch, with luck she should be back in the show ring quite quickly, particularly if she is a short-coated breed. Of course it takes much longer with a long-coated breed and the bitch could be out of the ring for anything up to six months and even more depending on the growth of the hair and how severely it was shed when she was nursing her litter. I have, however, known long-coated show bitches that have obviously been particularly well looked after during their motherhood come back into the ring in sparkling condition not long after they have been weaned from their puppies. Such dedication by their owners certainly deserves rich rewards.

5

Rearing puppies

The ability to rear puppies correctly is an important part of any breeder's programme, as without it losses can be heavy Some of the best whelps may be lost. Weaning is a very critical time in a puppy's life and if the transition from a mother's milk to more solid food is not done with the utmost care and regularity of feeding, digestive troubles can result. These will put the puppy back in its progress and it may take quite some time to get it right again. In the production of show dogs (and that is surely what all breeders are aiming at), rearing includes not only feeding but exercise and general care. Many experts, Veterinary Surgeons and experienced breeders, maintain that some of the abnormalities present in dogs today are due not so much to inheritance but to bad environmental conditions and incorrect rearing (see discussion of hip displasia, page 124).

The puppy which is the largest at birth does not always grow into the largest and strongest adult. A good puppy that is a slow maturer will in the great majority of cases turn out the best and will certainly keep its condition, make and shape longer than those that are ready at a very early age. Patience is certainly a very valuable attribute in rearing puppies.

There is little that one can do with a litter for the first two or three weeks if everything is going according to plan (dew claws and the docking of tails are dealt with in the previous chapter). Pay great attention to hygiene and keep the bitch and her whelping quarters immaculately clean. She will normally keep her puppies clean but you must watch for any irregularities that appear as the puppies advance in age. If they are continually crying there is something seriously wrong—it is distressing to watch them crawling around obviously very discontented. In this state they will not suck properly from the dam and even if you hold them onto a teat they are not strong enough to suck correctly. If you pick the puppy up it will feel cold and thin and with its plaintive cry it looks a pathetic little creature. You can imagine, to have several of her litter in such a state upsets the bitch enormously and quick action must be taken to try and sort out the infection. You may be lucky and save the stronger pups but the weaker puppies will usually die, particularly if there are signs of a yellowish diarrhoea. The common name used for this sort of trouble is 'fading puppies' but the cause can be one of many infections such as streptococcal, staphylococcal or E-coli infections. It is usually found in the passage from the mouth to the anus, the alimentary canal. Penbritin, which is a type of penicillin, can save the puppies if given early enough but the symptoms must be noticed before they become too deep-rooted. Bitches always seem to know when their whelps are not going to survive and they will discard them from the litter and even push them in behind their back no doubt hoping that out of sight is out of mind. I never believe in trying to revive a puppy that the bitch has discarded—she knows best in the end.

Puppies' ears are closed when they are born but usually start to open about the tenth day. Some long-coated breeds have a tendency for hair to grow in the ear canal and this must be plucked out as they grow. Do this very gently and only a few hairs at a time. Similarly, puppies' eyes are shut when they are born and generally start to open from about eight days onwards. The eye starts to open at the inside corner and gradually the opening spreads across the whole of the eye. Sometimes the eye appears to be a little sticky and unwilling to open. In such a case gently wipe from the inside corner with a little very weak Optrex and the crust that has formed should easily come away and the eye will open. Inspect such conditions of the eye regularly until you are quite sure that the eye is clean and healthy. Full vision does not come to a puppy until it is about five to six weeks old. It is thought that before that they can only really distinguish between light and dark. In the early stages I always feel that their nose tells them more than their eyes.

Puppies should grow in weight regularly and it is a good idea to weigh them twice a week, certainly for the first two weeks, and then once a week thereafter when you can be assured that a steady progress is being made. Provided they are happy, sucking well from their dam, putting on weight steadily and, when you lift them to be weighed, full of twists and turns, they are coming along very well and there is no need to worry.

Watch carefully at this time for any signs of imperfections. For example, you may have reason to think that one of the puppies is deaf and this happens in certain breeds. Drop a tin plate or something that will make a noise behind the puppy and if there is no reaction then your suspicions are probably justified. The only humane thing to do with this puppy is to put it down, as otherwise it would be living in a dangerous world with no warning of any impending danger; don't think that you are doing someone a good turn by passing on this puppy. It could bring tragedy into someone else's home. Sometimes a puppy is born with defective eyesight in one eye. Provided you explain this carefully to a would-be buyer and they are prepared to give the puppy a home knowing the imperfection then the puppy should manage adequately to cope with its infirmity.

If a puppy appears to have difficulty in holding on to a teat and does not seem to be gaining in weight check it for a cleft palate. This can run the entire length of the palate or it may extend only to a greater or lesser degree. The defect prevents the puppy forming a vacuum in its mouth; it is therefore quite unable to suck properly and milk is frequently seen coming down the nostrils. This defect is more common in the short-nosed breeds. These puppies should be put down at birth as although it may be possible to correct the condition surgically the congenital factor remains.

A hare lip often accompanies a cleft palate. With this condition, too, a puppy should be put down.

A puppy that grows up very much smaller and weaker than its brothers and sisters should never be passed on to a new home without having a very careful examination by a Veterinary Surgeon. This puppy may be suffering from various ailments, the most common of which is a bad or abnormal heart. It is far kinder to put this puppy to sleep as it will never catch up with its own kind, and although someone may be happy to give it a good home there is almost always heartache in the end. It is surely better to end the puppy's life when it is in your ownership. This may sound very hard but I have lived with dogs now for over 50 years and this advice is based on experience. Some special people really love to try and make weaklings into strong healthy puppies but it is rarely successful and the attempt can cause a great deal of sadness and heartache. The same applies to old dogs. I always feel that when an old dog is really unhappy it should be released from its unhappiness. We have the right to do this and we should not be cowardly about it.

It is fascinating to watch the young puppies grow and develop their own characters, and they are specially appealing when they learn to stand on their own four feet, between three and four weeks, and assert themselves. Little arguments develop with their brothers and sisters, with growling noises to express their feelings. At about this time the puppy's first teeth start to come through. These are the upper canines. The breeder begins to know them all individually and watches them carefully with a view to choosing puppies of show potential. Some breeders say that they like to pick their show prospects almost at birth. I am not an advocate of this as much can happen to a puppy from the time it is born until it is mature, and on the way up the breeder can have many bitter disappointments. From experience I know that just when you think you have the right puppy for the show ring and you can see it winning top awards, then, for some unaccountable reason, its teeth do not come in correctly or its tail curls too much, or its eyes are too light in colour. We should all have learned from such experiences and not be too anxious to pick our show prospects too soon.

The size of the litter must govern when the puppies should have supplementary feeding. If there is a large litter then obviously as soon as the babes are able to take solid food the better. In this case two weeks is not too young to try them with some very good scraped raw meat. I believe in allowing the bitch to rear her puppies as long as she seems able to and without causing her undue strain. Normally I do not start weaning the pups until three weeks. Put the raw meat on your finger and let the puppies suck it away from your finger. Watch you don't lose the tip of your finger! It is amazing how quickly they get the idea of this new food and they respond immediately. Their little noses twitch as they seem to get the scent of it and most breeds need very little encouragement. Repeat this performance for a few days and then give them two little lots of scraped meat each day, one in the morning and one in the afternoon. Gradually increase this until a plate of meat is put down for the whole family. Do watch the greedy feeders: there will always be one or two, and some get so anxious to have as much as possible that they even choke and someone must be on hand at this early stage to rescue them. The slower feeders must have more time to digest their allocation, and as the puppies get older it is better and fairer to give them all their own dishes. The dam will, of course, always be pleased to finish up anything that is left over.

When the puppies tuck into their meat heartily, introduce a very fine puppy meal that has been soaked in a good gravy. Having established two meat meals and a biscuit meal per day introduce the youngsters to their milk meals. These can be either a good puppy milk or a baby food cereal. I always find this to be the messiest business of the lot and the puppies seem to get it all over themselves to begin with. Never mind— they can be cleaned off or their litter mates will help to lick it off.

If the puppies are weaned gradually the bitch should not experience any difficulty in getting rid of her own milk and in helping her to do this you should be decreasing the quantity of food that she is given. Many bitches have a habit of regurgitating their food for their puppies. This will not hurt the pups and they are perfectly capable of digesting this part-digested food themselves.

At about three weeks of age the puppies should be wormed, as it would be most unusual if they did not have a good supply of roundworm, *Toxocara canis.* This type can, in very rare circumstances, be transmitted to children and cause blindness. It is at three weeks of age that the eggs which will have come from the dam will have become adult worms. These worms delay the progress of the pups and the sooner they are got rid of the better. They are threadlike in appearance, white in colour and a bit like a long piece of spaghetti with pointed ends. Ask your Veterinary Surgeon for the correct vermifuge and be sure that you give the right dose as directed. Puppies that are infested with worms have a dry unhealthy appearance to their coat and if you smell their breath it is distinctly unsavoury. Worms are usually excreted up to 24 hours after the dosage and if at all possible try to sweep them up before the bitch gets to them. You will, as already suggested, worm the bitch when she is finished with her puppies but the less she has to clean up in this respect the better. Make sure that you take these excreted worms to an incinerator or burn them on a fire as you do not want any possible chance of re-infection. While the bitch is cleaning up after her puppies she too is likely to pass worms and she must not be allowed to do this anywhere except in her own garden where you can dispose of them in the same way.

It is advisable to give the puppies a second worming dose at about six weeks of age and yet again at eight weeks if there are still signs that the puppies are harbouring worms. Worming with good preparations will not upset the puppies and it is advisable to ask the new owners of the puppies to worm them again at six months, then a year, and thereafter every year unless there are symptoms of worms being present. A dog with worms is not a healthy dog and you will never get a dog into super show condition if it is harbouring these pests.

KENNEL CLUB REGISTRATION

Kennel Club registration usually takes a little time, and it is best to send in the application to register the puppies when they are about four or five weeks old. At this age you can reasonably expect the litter to survive and therefore you are not wasting any money. Write to the Kennel Club (addresses at the end of the book) for an application for puppy registration and litter recording by the breeder. This form is self-explanatory and at the same time as registering the litter you can register by name any puppies that you so wish. The total number of puppies must be declared at the time of recording of the litter. If no puppies are named the fee is £5 plus £1 for each puppy in the litter. Therefore if you have a litter of six, three dogs and three bitches, and you intend to record the litter only, the fee is £11, £5 for litter recording plus £1 for each puppy not registered in the active register. If, however, you intend to name one or more puppies the fee will be £5 for each named puppy plus £1 for each puppy not named in the litter. These fees are correct at the time of writing, but are regularly revised.

It may be that as this is your very first litter, you will want to register them all, but most breeders today, because of the high cost, are inclined to register only the puppies that they think are of show standard.

The Kennel Club will return to you a registration card for all the puppies you have named and for the others you will be sent a form enabling the new owners to register the puppies in a name of their choice. These forms must be given to the new owners at the time of purchase as must be the registration cards for any named puppies. This registration card must be signed by you as the breeder on the line indicated. These Kennel Club forms must accompany the pedigree of the puppy at time of purchase plus, of course, the diet sheet and any special instructions that you may like to go forward with the puppy. There is quite a lot of paperwork involved in breeding dogs, and when you come on to showing them, there is even more.

The procedure for registration in the United States is very similar —apply to the American Kennel Club.

THE PUPPY AND A NEW HOME

Between seven and eight weeks the puppies should be completely weaned, having been wormed at least twice, and ready for their new homes. This is a very important time in the life of the puppy, when it is taken away from all its friends and familiar surroundings and kennel smells and transported to a new life altogether. Here it is likely to be on

47

its own with nothing but strange humans, large and small, around it. Do tell the new owners not to let the children, if there are any, overtax the puppy. Like children, the puppy must have its rest periods whilst it is still growing. Bringing a puppy up with children is a splendid thing and done properly it is good discipline for both sides.

Give the puppy every help by trying to make sure that the owners are suitable people to have a puppy, understand the requirements of the pup and are prepared to be guided by your diet sheet (see page 52) and general instructions. This particularly applies when the new owners are having a puppy for the very first time. I also always give them some basic training instructions for the puppy as even if they only half follow your suggestions it can help the puppy settle down and be a good member of the household.

The basic training of any puppy must consist of three things. He must learn to appreciate the difference between 'yes' and 'no'. He must learn to be clean in the house and he must learn his name. In training the puppy must never be confused by a long string of words and these words must be spoken in the manner that you mean. If this procedure is rigidly adhered to the puppy will soon know from the tone of voice whether he has been good or bad. The puppy must never be tormented or teased by the children. This can upset his training very considerably as he will be thoroughly confused and not know the difference between right and wrong. Be fair to him at all times and he will very soon respond and understand.

Once a name is chosen for the puppy it must be used at all times. He will soon realize that whatever name you have chosen belongs especially to him and he will respond to it. The vast majority of dogs want to please their masters and are delighted when they do.

When the puppy leaves your care at eight or ten weeks he really has only about three thoughts in his head. First must come food, secondly his fun and games and human companionship and thirdly having had enough of the first two he wants to settle down and sleep. It is the combination of these three things that should be used to educate and train the puppy. His rest is just as important as his playtime—he needs frequent rest periods to help restore the physical and mental energy that he is continually using up.

Explain to the new owners that the puppy should have his own toys such as a ball, marrow bone, old slipper or some such similar object but never, never chicken bones or similar bones that will splinter and cause internal damage. If he has his own toys there is no excuse for him to start chewing people's possessions no matter how tempting they may be. If found doing this he must be scolded, the object taken away from him and one of his own special possessions given to him instead. If he insists on going back to what does not belong to him he must be scolded each time he does it and here a tap on his bottom with a rolled-up newspaper can be very effective. A hand should never be used to scold the puppy as he looks upon his owner's hand as a friendly thing that comforts and pets him and that also feeds him. If he is scolded by being hit by his owner's hand he will quickly lose confidence in his new owner.

A word about night procedure can be helpful to a new owner. My advice is always that the puppy must learn that he has to spend time in his own bed wherever that may be situated. It is hopeless to take him up to the bedroom if he cries because he will very quickly learn that it is a much nicer place and he enjoys human company. Puppies, like children, can very quickly acquire bad habits that can be so difficult to break.

The basic training of any puppy is very important and as it must start at an early age it is advisable that only very elementary training be taught to the puppy at least until he has really established himself as part of the household. This training will not tire him unnecessarily as each little lesson will be of short duration.

When he has mastered being clean in the house, to recognize his own name and the meaning of yes and no, he will be well on his way to learning what a collar and lead means. Some puppies take to this quite naturally but one occasionally gets the stubborn pup that either behaves like a bucking bronco or digs his feet into the ground and refuses to move. I think the latter is the more difficult to cope with and requires great patience. Explain to the new owners that the best way to get the puppy accustomed to a collar before attaching the lead to it is to obtain a soft round collar, never a choke chain, and put it on once or twice each day for a brief period and always when they are around to watch what the puppy is doing. He may take no notice at all of this encumbrance but if he does and seems seriously to object to it then it is best to take it off; when he is having a few moments of petting put the collar on again and give him confidence by talking kindly to him, stroking his head and behind his ears and generally making a fuss of him. The puppy will soon forget that he has a collar on and come to accept it quite naturally.

Advise your new clients not to lift the puppy on to their knee for petting. His place should be quite firmly on the floor and they must bend down to talk to him. It should be remembered that in the early stages he is a small thing but, depending on the breed, he will grow and once given the opportunity to sit on chairs or laps he will not forget about this readily and it will not be so funny when he dives in from the garden wet and dirty and lands straight in the middle of the best settee or a clean suit or dress. The habit of climbing on to laps turns into one of jumping up at people and this is certainly something to be avoided.

It is of the utmost importance that you tell the new owners of the necessity to have the puppy injected against hard pad, distemper, hepatitis, and leptospirosis. This can be done when the puppy is 10–12 weeks old, and consists of two injections a fortnight apart. Having the injections done at this time gives the youngster an opportunity to settle in his or her new home before being subjected to the needle. In fact, few feel anything at all and it is rare that they suffer any after-effects.

In view of the recent outbreak of parvo-virus, canine enteritis, it is advisable to recommend your clients to have the puppy inoculated against it. Ask them to consult with their Veterinary Surgeon as to the best time to have the puppy fully covered. Veterinary Surgeons have slightly different views on this subject and they also differ as to what they consider the best coverage for parvo-virus. There is a live vaccine and a dead vaccine and both seem to have been very successful.

Make sure that you have told the new owners that until the puppy is injected they must not let it out of its own surroundings; they must not imagine that it would be nice for the new puppy to have some company and invite the neighbour's dog in to say hello. Infection can be lurking round the corner and having just purchased a healthy puppy from you the new owners must not take any risks, even though it is very tempting to take the new puppy to show off to friends. It is only a little period to wait until the puppy is fully covered by inoculations. Do advise them to be patient—it will be well worth while in the end.

Puppies have a natural immunity against these virus infections from their mother and this lasts up to about 9 to 10 weeks. It is fortunate that because of science and research we are able to protect them further and booster doses of the various vaccines should be given to the dogs every year until in their older age they should be largely immune. Very few boarding kennels today will accept dogs that are not inoculated; and if they do, you can be slightly suspicious that their kennel management is not of the high standard that you should be looking for.

If your client wishes you to keep the puppy until he is fully injected, and there could be very good reasons for this, it is always better to get the Veterinary Surgeon to send the account direct to your client and you, of course, must charge board for the extra weeks that you are keeping the puppy. We much prefer that the new owners take the puppy at about eight weeks and take it to their own Veterinary Surgeon to have its course of injections. This also allows them to have it checked by the Veterinary Surgeon and if there is something that you have not noticed it can be sorted out straight away.

Recently a lady who had purchased a bitch puppy from me telephoned in a fury to say that she had been sold a dog. She told us that she had even taken it to the local pet shop and they had confirmed that it was a dog. She emphatically told my husband on the phone that the bitch had a 'little willie' as she called it, attached to it! She was instructed to bring the puppy back and this she did within an hour or so accompanied by granny and husband. The kennel staff were hysterical about the whole affair; when she arrived it was confirmed that she had in fact been sold what she had wanted, i.e. a bitch puppy. She was then taken down to the kennels to be shown the difference between the sexes and have her education completed. Breeding dogs is certainly not without its humour!

When the puppies have all gone to their new homes, except perhaps for the one or two that may look promising for the show ring, the puppy house and run should be thoroughly disinfected before the introduction of another litter. The same applies to the whelping box; there is a very good disinfectant on the market today designed specifically for the job.

THE DIET SHEET

Space does not allow me here to give detailed set diets for particular breeds; naturally the diet for a Chihuahua or a Yorkshire Terrier will differ very considerably from that of an Irish Wolfhound or Great Dane. Breeders vary in their recommendations for feeding even within a breed but as all good breeders will supply a diet sheet it is best to continue along the lines suggested so that there are no interruptions to the normal development of the puppy. Wise and sensible feeding plays a very great part in the growth of any young animal; it also helps to produce a disease-resistant constitution and too much emphasis cannot be put on this very important matter. Any correct diet should consist of two-thirds good protein, i.e. meat, fish, eggs and milk plus one-third carbohydrates, such as meal, cereals, biscuits. Add to this supplementary minerals in the form of calcium and phosphorus and you should have the right result. Protein foods produce the essential amino-acids which in their turn help form the antibodies which are an animal's defence mechanism against disease.

Incorrect feeding can do much to ruin the finished picture of the adult dog. It can considerably weaken the bone, the dog's stamina and its resistance to disease and even parasites. It can also produce a certain amount of unsoundness due to the imperfect development of bone and muscle in certain parts of the body. What a puppy grows into as an adult can depend almost as much on its feeding and rearing (including environment) as on its breeding. To rear a puppy on a deficient diet will never bring success and will not ensure that the maximum bone growth is made between the time of weaning and maturity. This does not mean that puppies should be allowed to become grossly fat and overweight. If this happens it can so easily affect the bone as with a heavy plump body the immature limbs are just not strong enough to hold up this frame; they become bent and rather bowed and elbows jut out. These faults, once appearing, are very difficult to get rid of and show stock can so very easily be ruined in this way.

A puppy's diet should be watched carefully at all times so that the end-product is a youngster that is nicely rounded without in any way being pot-bellied or lumpy. One very often finds that if a puppy is kept too fat it will go off its food at four or five months of age; and at this time in its growth it is vitally important that it should have steady, uninterrupted growth, without days of fasting and being fussy about what it eats. These days can do much harm to the puppy.

I give below a specimen diet sheet that I have used now for over 30 years and which has produced for me all my many Champions and show stock. Feeding in kennels has, of course, its advantages. One has a separate refrigerator and deep freezer for the dogs. I would never like to suggest that anyone tries to keep raw uncleaned tripe in their household refrigerator. This will very quickly taint everything else with its own strong odour, an odour that the dogs certainly seem to relish. Raw tripe for dog consumption needs a home of its own and because of this it may well be that you would prefer to substitute one of the very well known brands of prepared food which are available from most large stores or pet shops.

Diet sheet for Labrador/Golden Retriever/Boxer size of dogs
Note: Naturally, for the smaller breeds the quantities must be cut down and for the bigger

dogs increased.

From 8 to 14 weeks of age
8 a.m.   6oz of raw meat or raw tripe plus a fine biscuit meal soaked in a good gravy. (Never feed unsoaked meal as it can swell up inside the dog and cause severe digestive problems.)
12 noon   About a cupful of cereal made with hot or cold milk depending on the weather. This can be either cow's milk or goat's milk. The latter is excellent for rearing puppies as it is nearest in composition to the bitch's milk.
4 p.m.   As at 8 a.m.
8 p.m.   Hot or cold milk.

14 weeks to 6 months
8 a.m.   8oz of raw meat or tripe plus a medium biscuit meal soaked in a good gravy
12 noon   Bowl of cereal made with hot or cold milk plus the addition, twice a week, of a raw egg.
6 p.m.   As at 8 a.m.

6 months to 1 year
8 a.m.   8–10oz of raw meat or tripe plus a good dog meal soaked in gravy
12 noon   A small drink of milk if the dog wants it
6 p.m.   As at 8 a.m.

From 14 weeks onwards I have always added a pinch of bone meal powder suitable for animal consumption. This I continue to give until the animal is fully mature and the quantity grows from a pinch at 14 weeks up to a good desertspoonful for the bigger dogs as they mature.

Some puppies will eat more biscuit meal than others without becoming too fat and some will hardly touch it at all and be rather inclined to pick at it. Individual dogs vary very much, and of course there are great variations from breed to breed.

The meal times can be adjusted to suit your own personal convenience but do be sure that the times are the same every day and when the dog is adult and having only one meal a day it is very important that it should be given at the same time each day.

It is as well to know the sources of the various vitamins:

Vitamin A: fish-liver oils, liver and eggs.
Vitamin B: liver, yeast and the germ of cereals.
Vitamin C: citrus fruits.
Vitamin D: liver, butter and fish-liver oils.
Vitamin E: wheatgerm oil.
Vitamin K: essential for blood clotting.

Rearing puppies

Vitamin D is also manufactured naturally in the skin by the action of sunlight, hence the value of sunlight for young growing puppies.

The exact composition of a bitch's milk does vary but the following table gives an average composition (in per cent).

	Water	Sugar	Fat	Casein	Albumin	Mineral Ash
Bitch	75.1	3.2	9.8	6.1	5.1	0.7
Cow	87.0	4.7	3.9	3.0	0.7	0.7
Goat	86.7	4.5	3.9	3.2	1.0	0.7

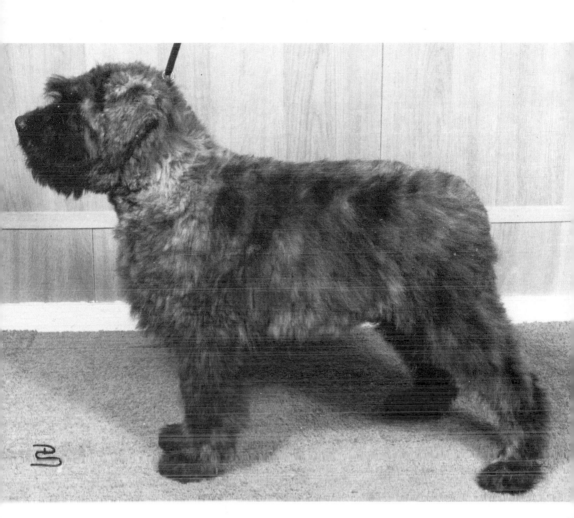

Exciting young Bouvier des Flandres, three
months of age and in good show stance

ABOVE
A Beagle bitch at six months and maturing nicely

LEFT
The correct scissor bite

A professional handler prepares a West Highland White Terrier. The chalk must be completely brushed out of the coat before the dog enters the ring

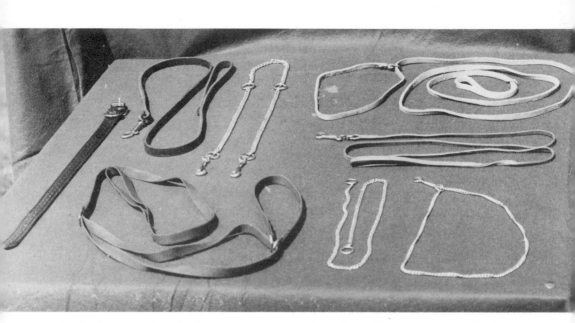

A selection of leads and collars

Grooming equipment: top, two-sided brush, wire and bristle; centre left to right, hound glove, single-sided stripping blade, double-sided stripping blade, fine metal comb, good all-round comb, medium comb, wire slicker brush; bottom, trimming scissors and curved scissors as used for the removal of dew claws

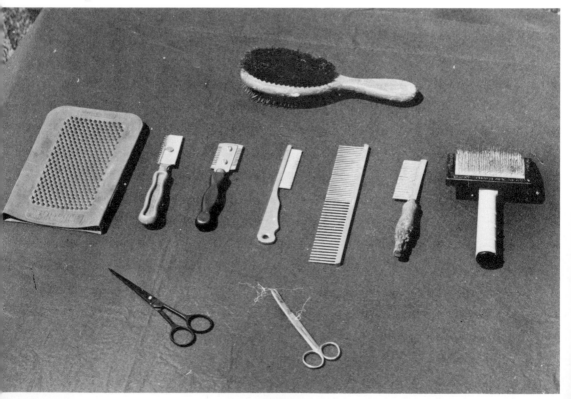

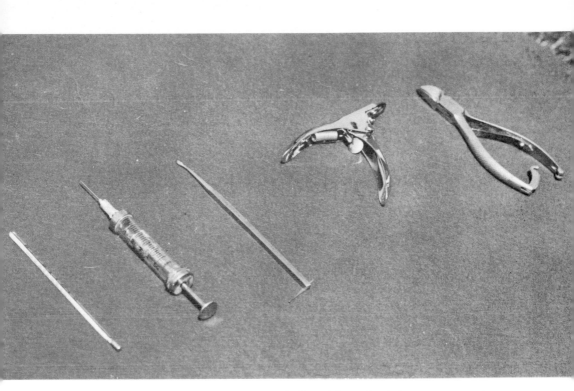

Left to right, animal thermometer, syringe, tooth scaler, and two types of nail clippers

LEFT
The strains of exhibition beginning to show! Dogs that are campaigned too heavily do get fed up with showing

RIGHT
Handling with a loose lead, and the dog standing quite naturally

BELOW
Tight lead handling, as used with many of the Terrier breeds

Benches are a must for all General
Championship Shows in Great Britain; in
America, very few shows are benched

Above A Pointer head *Right* Golden
Retriever head

These two photographs show the correct
types of head, and what judges should be
looking for in these breeds

A good Poodle head with, obviously, a good
length of tongue

6

Choosing a show puppy

Choosing the best show prospects in a litter is not an easy task, and strangely enough those that think it is have often been proved not to be the best at it! At six weeks a puppy can look an absolute little model of what you want when it is fully mature. Excitement rises high and although one should know better because of previous disappointments, one automatically begins to pin high hopes on this star of the future. At about three months in the smaller breeds and slightly older in the larger breeds, the puppy goes through a phase which we term, in the dog game, a 'legs and wings' stage. This means that it has become gangly, rather loose and un-coordinated, and often the body does not seem to fit the legs or head. In fact the overall picture of the puppy as it is at this stage makes one wonder why on earth one ever thought it could possibly be a show prospect. This is a most depressing and difficult time to try and assess show puppies. I personally do not look at them too critically during this period as experience has shown that, if the pedigree and the various dogs in it are known to be good, with that essential little bit of luck in most cases the puppy will grow out of this ugly stage and revert to being a show prospect.

While some breeders are very good at picking their show prospects, others seem to be quite hopeless and one has to wonder if they have an eye for a dog at all. Some breeders are far better at rearing their puppies than others but even these good rearers can fall sadly short in choosing their best ones. It is a very important part of a dog breeder's programme, and this art is to be valued and cherished by those fortunate enough to possess it. In puppy classes at shows which include puppies from six to twelve months of age, very exciting classes to judge, the judge is judging, or should be judging, as he or she sees the particular puppy on that day and not on what the puppy might mature into. For instance although the make and shape of a particular puppy may seem right in a judge's eye its head could be untypical of the breed at six or even nine months of age. If this is so that puppy can hardly be expected to win top honours and no doubt the breeder, who should know the weakness in the puppy, will only have taken the puppy to the show to get ring experience and to get to know what showing is all about. The breeder should have sufficient confidence in his/her own stock to know that the puppy's head will mature along the right lines and come right in the end and so be prepared to give the puppy the occasional outing to educate it for its future show career. There is, of course, always the risk that some judge will report on the puppy and at British shows, give him a bad critique which can stay with him, so often unjustly, for too long a period and do his show career untold harm.

Let us explain this question of critiques. These are written by the judges for the two British dog papers, *Dog World* and *Our Dogs*, and submitted the week after judging. The reports are quite an onerous task for judges, particularly during the busy show season when senior judges are officiating most weeks and often twice in one week. Britain is the only country in the world where these reports are printed for everyone to read, not only in Britain, but right round the globe where the papers are very eagerly awaited. Unfortunately the standard of these reports is not always worthy of the publicity that they receive. It is very puzzling to read in one report that an authority considers that a certain dog has a good head typical for the breed and a few weeks later that the same dog was referred to by another judge at another show as untypical in head. I have even known dogs' eyes to change in colour from week to week! This makes one wonder if the judges have been judging the same dog and even more important what value there can possibly be in such critiques.

With experience one knows which critiques one can rely on; these knowledgeable and constructive reports are very much appreciated and can be most helpful particularly to overseas people who so often rely on them for reports on dogs that they may be considering purchasing.

As we have already said, the Kennel Club in each country issue Standards for all breeds and you will no doubt have read and re-read the standard that refers to your bitch and almost be able to quote it verbatim. You must now try to apply it to your puppies in miniature and there is no doubt that experience in this field is a very valuable asset. The novice breeder has so much to find out but provided he or she is prepared to learn, picking the best in a litter is one of the most exciting facets of the dog game. To do it properly calls for constant critical inspection as you watch the youngsters go through their various phases; in aiming to keep the best you must also be able to discard for the pet market, as a kennel has to rely on these very important pet sales to produce an income and so help support the show stock.

Competition is so keen in the show ring today that it is quite useless to keep anything but one's very best stock. From a financial angle it is just as cheap (or expensive, depending on how one looks at it), to keep and feed a good dog as it is a not-so-good dog.

If the standard of your dog demands that it requires good bone and substance there is no sense in keeping a dog that does not have this as a youngster as it is very unlikely, no matter how much you feed the puppy, that it will suddenly develop this at a later date. On the other hand if the standard demands that a breed should have a dainty frame with almost fragile bone then it is useless to keep a heavy boned puppy that would never fine down even if you starved him, and you would hardly want to do that. Colour is an easy one to cope with as if a colour is banned in the standard, e.g. white in Boxers, then the best thing to do is to have the whelp put down at the time of birth. Dalmations are born white and the spots come afterwards. Pulis are born with ordinary hair and the cording does not start to come until they are about six months. These are all elementary facts, which you can read about in a book that is written for a particular breed, facts that you can learn all about also by talking to the breeders of your chosen breed.

There is no safe, hard and fast method for choosing your best puppy to keep for showing. Even the experts have made wrong decisions on occasions. Some have been fortunate to buy back puppies that were sold as pets but turned out well as they matured. Others have been less fortunate and have had to rely on the pleasure of seeing other people win with stock they have bred and allowed to 'escape'. Many breeders, of course, sell show stock and revel in the advertisement that show success brings to the kennel and I have to admit that it gives most of us tremendous pleasure to see others win with stock we have bred. Few kennels can keep all the show stock that they produce which shows that many kennels are breeding to a very good type and their breeding programme has a very sound foundation. The minority breed and show inferior stock and just do not seem to be able to raise the standard of their dogs, which suggests that they are not breeding along the correct lines.

Let me try to help you sort out your puppies through their most important stages. Some people maintain that they can pick their show puppies at birth. I certainly do not go along with this assertion. I wish I could because it would save a great deal of money in 'running on' puppies that could have been sold as pets at eight weeks. A puppy which is 'run on' is categorized as a show prospect and will be kept for further observation and selection.

At three months of age one should be able to recognize whether or not the lay-back of the shoulder is correct and whether the dog is likely to be long in back or loin. You will see from any illustrated diagram the various points of the dog and be able to compare them with what should apply to your particular breed. If a puppy appears long in the back he might shorten a little with maturity but he will never be a short-backed animal and if the standard demands that he should be I would think again about keeping him. I always feel, however, that a bitch should be allowed that little bit of extra length of back because of maternal duties.

Some people claim that by eight weeks they can tell whether a puppy is worthy of being labelled a show prospect. I think that at that age one *can* certainly be fairly sure about particular anatomical points of con-formation, such as the length of back, lay-back of shoulders, wide or narrow front etc., and it is usually at this age that I like to put my show prospects to one side, watch them carefully, and try to predict their future development. Temperament is a very important factor in a show dog as without it life for both handler and dog can be anything but pleasant. At the eight-week stage one can readily see whether or not a puppy is going to be an outgoing happy dog or whether it is going to cringe at the slightest noise and not favour any human approach. Can you imagine a show dog backing away from the judge? Some do and they get no prize cards. Shy temperaments can be helped but it is usually a very uphill job and the dog tends to let one down when it should be doing its best to show off its virtues. Bad temperaments should really never be considered in dogs at all but certainly not in a show dog. Dogs that show any resentment of a judge handling them by trying to bite the judge are usually ordered from the ring and quite rightly so. Never forget also that this can be a hereditary trait and should not be bred from.

At the eight-week stage one cannot with any degree of certainty assess tail carriage, ear carriage and length and texture of coat. To be sure about these points one must wait until the puppy reaches the age of about six months. On some breeds one can tell earlier, but to be absolutely sure one needs these extra few weeks.

This also applies in many cases to heads as they can change quite dramatically in some breeds during puppyhood and that means anything up to 12 months of age. In those breeds that require a definite 'stop', i.e., a deep depression below the eyebrows, this can take time to mould but experienced breeders who know their own type of head will be fairly certain that the head will mature along the right lines if the head is right for type at birth and in the early days of the whelp's existence. On this point experienced breeders can be very helpful to the novice if a stud dog from their kennel has been used.

In Beagles at birth I like to see my whelps with a very strong head, a miniature St Bernard head, and this particularly applies to the dog puppies. If at eight weeks one can still find this head on the whelps I can be reasonably sure that they will finish up with good heads. These puppies are then put to one side to grow on and mature, we hope, in the right way and they are watched very carefully while they play and move around their kennel. I hope that their early good points, which have warranted their selection as show prospects, will continue to develop; if any faults appear and they are serious enough the puppies concerned will automatically be discarded and sold as pets.

Conformation is all-important in show dogs as without it the movement of the dog cannot be right; but do not be over-hasty in this matter. Always remember that as the young hopeful grows on he could, as explained earlier, go through a bad stage of being rather unco-ordinated in his movement; for example he might tend to come towards one throwing his elbows around a bit or not using his hocks properly. Time and correct exercise should rectify this; by correct exercise I mean *controlled exercise* on a lead at a steady pace that will make him use himself properly and not allow him to be slovenly and sloppy. The sort of exercise required differs in all breeds and must not be overdone as it is just as bad to tire the dog with too much exercise as it is not to give him enough. In a book of this description it is not possible to list all the breeds with the correct exercise at the different stages of growth, but it should be detailed in the many specialist books. Such exercise is a very important part of your rearing programme, more important perhaps than most realize.

We have not talked about mouths and dentition: this is a very important area in most breeds, and certainly in these early stages. In most gundogs, hounds and terriers the standard demands either that the mouth should be a scissor bite, when the upper incisors just overlap and touch the outer surface of the lower incisors, or that it should have a level bite. In some other breeds not in the above groups an undershot bite is required, such as in a Boxer. This means that the lower incisors project beyond the upper incisors. If such a bite is stipulated it is quite useless to present a dog in the show ring with a mouth that does not fit this standard. One tooth out of place, to most judges, is not a disqualification, but just one small point in the overall animal; but a mouth that is wrongly set should be heavily penalized. For instance a wry jaw, when the lower jaw is tilted to one side or another and is not parallel with the upper jaw, is a serious fault in most breeds and some judges will not tolerate it.

Some breeds have more trouble than others with regard to their dentition and it is not until their second or permanent teeth are through that one can safely put them into the show category. These teeth do not start to come through until nearly four months of age and although the milk teeth may have been placed quite correctly it does not always follow in some breeds that the permanent teeth will follow suit. This can be very disappointing to the breeder, particularly so if you previously thought that your line was completely free of any teeth problems and then one of these undesirable recessive genes makes itself known and upsets your applecart. It happens to us all and it could happen to you no matter how careful you think you have been, and it always affects the best puppy in the litter, or so it seems!

Eyes are fairly easy to assess, certainly for shape, and at ten weeks of age this should present no problem. Some breeds, such as Irish Water Spaniels, can darken in eye colour with maturity, but normally an eye which is light in a puppy will remain so. If your standard demands that the eye should be dark and it is very light, the fault can be seen straight away by all judges. Although it is only one aspect of the dog taken as a whole, it is a very noticeable point particularly if the sun is shining into the eyes. If the dog is a really top-class specimen in all other respects the problem is perhaps worth battling on with in the show ring but otherwise I would think twice before campaigning such a dog.

It is very important that puppies you consider to be show prospects should be given a few moments' training each day. I usually start this about 12 weeks of age when the puppy has been fully inoculated. At the same time I start lead training; with some breeds, if this day is put off you will have great difficulty in getting them to become at all civilized on a lead. I find the toys and some of the smaller terrier breeds the most difficult and obstinate to train. One Griffon that was my constant companion never did take to the lead and you can imagine the look that was given to me if I even dared try.

Whether it be on a table or on the ground, depending on the size of the breed, show prospects should be given the opportunity, early on, of learning the art of showing themselves off and great patience is required for this exercise. Pose them in a correct stance and praise them if they stay put and you will find that they take to it very readily. They are very appealing as they stand up like a little model and without moving their head turn their eyes to watch one as they are set up. Good show dogs are conceited even at an early age and I always feel it is a very hopeful sign if they have this rather proud, almost affected attitude.

In posing up your youngster you will quickly be able to tell about feet. If a cat foot is required it is no good hoping that a hare-foot will grow into a cat foot. In the vast majority of cases good feet are born. They can be helped along to look better by correct exercise but you will never *make* a good foot. If there is a weakness here think twice before keeping the puppy as a show possible.

Ears require to be correctly set according to the requirements for the standard of that breed. Ears that do not tip over as they should, for example as in Shetland Sheepdogs and Rough Collies, will not be acceptable just as ears in so many of the terrier breeds that should be upright and erect will gain no marks whatsoever for falling down like that of a hound. Ears are very important as they can impart to the head the expression that is typical of the breed. So often judges will make sharp little noises to attract the dog and make him listen, and in doing so assess the value of the ear in relation to the overall head. Dogs must learn to use their ears properly and in breeds where ear carriage is important the judge will, without doubt, check this carefully. A dead ear, i.e. one that does not respond to any noise, can spoil a dog's chances of winning top placings. When a puppy is teething ear carriage can be affected, and therefore before finally discarding a youngster because of bad ear carriage, it is best to wait until the puppy has his or her full complement of teeth. At six months of age ear carriage should be settling down to what the standard of that breed describes. In some countries — including North America and the Scandinavian countries — certain breeds are still allowed to have cropped ears. This is carried out when the puppy is about 12 weeks old, and so the problem of ear carriage does not arise in these cases.

Coats can be a problem, particularly with regard to texture; if the standard demands that the coat should be of a harsh texture, it is pointless to show a dog with a soft coat. If the standard says that the coat should be smooth, don't present a rough coat and hope to win.

Tails can be difficult as with maturity some dogs carry their tails too gaily and this spoils the whole outline of the dog. Very often the tail carriage of stud dogs will tend to be a little on the gay side, but this, in my opinion, is understandable as they are rightly confident about themselves; it can perhaps be excused as it is an expression of self-importance and almost dominance. Some breeds need tails to be tightly curled over the back and not to one side or the other. If the tail is slack and falls to one side, this again is undesirable. It is no good having a merry little Cocker with a tail stuck firmly down with no sign of life. A tail certainly helps to express any dog's character. I once judged a Chow that kept wagging his tail at me but when I went to judge him he wanted to bite me! I am sure there is a moral here somewhere.

All these points are over and above the make and shape of the body of the dog itself according to the standard. Then there is the question of 'quality'. 'Quality' in livestock has always been very difficult to describe; it is the one thing that lifts a good dog out of the ordinary category and puts him into a higher sphere altogether. If a dog has all the other virtues of his breed plus quality, that elusive, indefinable something which includes personality and character, a high grade excellence, then that dog should be destined for top honours.

The show dog must be capable of standing up to the rigours of show days and the very tiring travelling to and from the shows. Naturally exhibitors give their show stock every care and consideration but even so there are long days, sometimes nights too, away from home and they must be rather special dogs to put up with all this inconvenience. The great majority of show dogs do love their outings and this is particularly noticeable when the veterans are brought out to show their paces. They are thrilled to be back, they know what it is all about, and they show off. It is rewarding to judge a Veteran Class, the only trouble being that one wants to give a prize to them all and, in fact, they seem to expect it.

Think about all these things very carefully before trying to decide on your show stock. I hope that the foregoing will have been helpful to you but there is nothing like practical experience. There is no infallible procedure to pick the best pup in each litter but common sense and a strict adherence to your idea of the official Standard should help you reach your goal. Read as much about your breed as possible, talk to the breeders about it and store away all the knowledge that you can accrue. Watch your puppies grow up through all their different stages and do not be afraid to sell them all if they do not come up to what you consider show standard for your particular breed. It is only by being absolutely ruthless in your selection of show stock that you will be successful. You may have one or two disappointments at the beginning—we have all had them and not only at the beginning—but if you are dedicated to the breeding of better stock you will succeed in the end.

7

Running a kennel

In the successful kennel, as in other trades or professions, good management is essential. It is only through very detailed planning and overall organization of the kennel that success is likely to come your way. It is, for example, of the utmost importance that a very high degree of hygiene is maintained and this particularly applies when a breeding kennel is run in conjunction with a boarding kennel. Nowadays in Britain such kennels have to be approved by the local authority. All of us who have been involved in running such establishments have welcomed this restriction as it has helped to discourage unsuitable kennels which have been a source of infection and offered generally unsatisfactory conditions. In the following paragraphs I refer to the regulations as they apply in Britain. In America the rules are if anything even stricter, and you should investigate them fully before you start.

The ideal site for a kennel is one that has no near-neighbours who are likely to object to the noise of the dogs because, believe you me, there are those that choose to be quiet all day but howl all night. This is particularly true of the boarding dogs. It is not until you have accepted them into your care that you realize just what a problem they can be. If you intend to combine breeding with boarding it is essential, nevertheless, that the kennel be near enough a reasonably well-populated area where you can hope to recruit your clients. It should be easily accessible by road and if possible near some public transport.

If you are starting from scratch—perhaps not a very wisely chosen word in this context . . . let us say, if you are starting from the beginning and purchasing a property do make sure that the local authorities have no objections to your scheme; in no way enter into any agreement to purchase the property until written permission has been received from the planning authorities of the area concerned. It would be a catastrophe to go through with a purchase and then discover that your plans are frustrated by officialdom. Having got your initial planning permission, each year thereafter you will be required to fill in an application for your licence in accordance with the Animal Boarding Establishment Act of 1963. This is granted by your local authority and each year a representative from their Health Department and perhaps a Veterinary Surgeon will call to inspect your premises before re-issuing the licence. This system really safeguards all good breeding and boarding kennels as it ensures that only those that pass the necessary standards will be allowed to operate.

If you intend to purchase an already established kennel then the above licence should only require to be transferred from the seller to the new owner. This should be clearly established at the time of purchase and I personally would also prefer to have an impartial Veterinary report on the premises and any stock that you may be intending to take over. This would safeguard you, as it may be that the kennel has recently had some sort of epidemic such as kennel cough or a more serious virus infection. It is also wise to check that there have been no serious skin troubles as these have a habit of lingering on in the kennels. In any case if you are taking over kennel buildings it is sensible to treat all the kennels with one of the good disinfectants that are on the market specially for the prevention of these various complaints. If you do not start with a clean sheet it is likely that you will be harbouring trouble for the future.

Many breeding kennels have started in a small way and accepted the puppies that they have bred back as boarders when the owners had to be away from home. From these little beginnings they have grown and as the boarders help pay for the breeding stock boarding can be a great help financially; although at the end of a season when one takes time to assess the broken kennels, the chewed doors, the fencing that needs renewing or repairing, one does sometimes ask if it is really worthwhile. Of course one has repairs that need doing even with one's own stock, but nothing like the damage done by a dog that is determined to escape, objecting to being shut up in a strange kennel.

Kennels that are used for the boarding of dogs must be very strong and very safe and no kennel should be so made that it opens into an unfenced yard or paddock. I find Labrador Crosses to be one of the very best at ruining even the strongest kennel—it is incredible what damage they can do in a very short space of time. Dogs that are perfectly good at home and would not dream of chewing their bed can be the worst offenders in the boarding kennel. It is often no good trying to tell the owner how naughty they have been—owners just do not believe that their pet Sambo could be so impossible and the boarding kennel proprietor is just 'exaggerating'. Some dogs make up their mind right from the word go that the object of being in a boarding kennel is to escape and if you watch them quite unobserved one can almost see them planning their operations. Six-foot chain link is nothing to these dogs and it is absolutely essential that every boarding kennel should have several escape proof kennels, almost prisons, for the control of these renegades.

Most dogs are delighted to welcome their owners when they return. There are great leaps of joy and wagging tails and great reunions take place but on the other hand there are the odd one or two that seem to have preferred kennel life, and keep looking back longingly at their temporary home. Dogs quite obviously have their own way of communicating to each other and I always try to pair them together in kennels so that no dog is left on his own. There are some dogs, of course, that just will not accept a companion and they have to live their holiday, if that it be, on their own with only the occasional visits from the kennel staff. Some, I feel, miss their canine companions when they go home particularly if they are the only dog in the household. I would never keep one solitary dog; and I know from long experience that dogs do like a companion of their own kind. A pair of dogs produce much more fun for themselves and for the human family. At present I have a black Labrador and a Griffon as house pets. They play well together, and obviously adore each other, and amuse us by their antics.

Drinking buckets and feeding bowls should always be made of metal, which is easy to wash out in boiling water. Plastic bowls soon get chewed and it is never good for the dogs to swallow any of the chewed bits. Collars, particularly choke chains, should never be left on in kennels. Accidents can so easily happen if the dog happens to get his collar caught and in his attempts to get free twists round and round—very quickly one has a choked dog. Be warned: this is a very real danger both for your own stock and for a visiting animal and it is no good being sorry after the event.

When accepting dogs for boarding it is absolutely essential that before they are admitted to the kennel one is completely satisfied that they are in good health. A quick inspection at the time of admission can save a lot of bother later on. It is also very important that the dog is checked for fleas, lice or other mites and if the dog is found to have such visitors the owner should be told straight away. If they are not noticed on arrival, but are spotted when the dog leaves, the owner will not be amused and will certainly not believe that the dog came in with them.

It is really quite surprising what condition some dogs arrive in and even more surprising that the owners have not noticed. This particularly applies to the coated dogs and they themselves must feel uncomfortable and unhappy with their condition. Some dogs that come in to be clipped are so bad that the best thing that we can do for them is to take their coat right off just like a sheep. How can people keep dogs in such a bad condition without noticing that they are anything but comfortable? Some have these poor creatures in their bedroom, even sharing their bed! It makes my skin creep even to think about it.

All dogs should have a certificate from their Veterinary Surgeon to show that they have been fully injected for hard pad, distemper, virus hepatitis, leptospirosis and parvo-virus. No dog should be admitted unless fully covered. One cannot safeguard dogs in kennels too carefully and it can be pointed out to one's clients that such a requirement is for their own dog's welfare as well as for that of the kennel owner and all the other inmates. It is far better to turn away uninoculated animals rather than have the catastrophe of having to close the kennels down due to an epidemic. Think also of the possible loss to your breeding stock —which has perhaps taken you many years to build up. Never take the risk.

In boarding kennels a record of each dog admitted must be kept and many kennels prefer to do this in co-operation with an insurance company that insures the dog during the period of his stay and issues an insurance cover note. A copy of this insurance cover is given to the owner and the owner is requested to sign the form that is retained in kennels. On this form there is such information as the owner's name and address, where he or she will be while on holiday or during the absence from home, the breed, date of birth etc. of the animal and any special information with regard to diet and the like that may be helpful to the kennel owner. Owners are asked to produce their copy of this cover note when they come to collect their animal and this stops any unauthorized person attempting to make off with another's dog.

If we have a visiting bitch for one of our stud dogs the same hard-and-fast rules apply with regard to inoculations. She is housed in a special block of kennels for in-season bitches and although she can see other bitches through chain-link fencing she is never put with any other bitch in season. Bitches are very sensitive at this time and it is safer and easier to keep them on their own as the duration of their stay is usually very limited. Kennels for in-season bitches must be absolutely fool-proof as if they escape at this crucial time the result can be disastrous, something that should never happen in a well-organized kennel.

If a dog does escape from kennels it is usually quite useless to try and take up the chase. This generally just makes the animal all the more determined to get further away. However, it is well worth a lot of patience to get the dog safely back. In any case the Police must be informed, as well as any animal welfare society within reach and any other kennel in the neighbourhood. The owner must be contacted—the address should be in the booking-in book. If the owner is in the country it could be that he would like to come back and try to find the animal himself. If the owners is abroad he should still be informed and it is also a good plan to advise his neighbours just in case the dog returns to his own home.

In cases of sickness your Veterinary Surgeon should be called at all times. A complaint that older dogs very often suffer from in kennels is nephritis. Kidneys in older animals are often weak and a change of home and food is just enough to trigger off this condition. In nervous dogs a wet eczema can run riot and the poor dog can be covered with this skin complaint in no time at all. Sickness should be reported to the owners as soon as possible unless they are abroad when they have probably left someone else's address to get in touch with in an emergency.

A boarding kennel can certainly help to balance the books if properly controlled and organized, and it can so easily produce that extra bit of cash that is necessary to sustain a breeding and showing kennel. Very few breeding kennels make enough money for the owner to live on, even reasonably, and the same applies if it is a show kennel as well—this usually goes hand-in-hand with breeding. The cost of showing and all its many accompaniments is very high today and often puppies are sold far below their true value simply because it is cheaper in the end to let a puppy go at 8 or 10 weeks rather than feed it for some extra weeks and get no more value for it in the end.

The costing of running a kennel is not easy to estimate. It is only through very careful management that the kennel survives and establishes a good reputation for producing good stock. The successful kennel rightly guards its reputation jealously and pursues a policy of careful planning, patience and the determination to survive the many setbacks that can easily come its way. The demand for stock from a well known winning show kennel, large or small, will always be very much higher than that from an unknown source, just as the price of good stock is bound to be more than that of inferior stock.

By combining a breeding kennel with a boarding kennel each can help the other if sensibly managed. Staff from one can overlap into the other particularly during the quiet season in the boarding kennel. Food can be bought cheaper in bulk, as can kennel equipment. Each section can play its part in a successful larger enterprise.

II

Kennel
Clubs,
Shows
and Showing

8

Presenting, preparing & training show dogs

In the world of dog showing presentation and training of dogs is of the utmost importance. As the standard of competition is very high today it is imperative that one presents one's dog as well as possible. Dog show entries have continued to increase, particularly at the Championship Shows, even at a time of economic recession on both sides of the Atlantic. With this great support from exhibitors dog shows themselves are becoming more professional each year, and the dogs are better presented and handled than they were in the past.

All this is good for our sport but it does make show success more difficult for dogs that are not presented well, and not trained properly for the show ring. It is a sad fact, that because they cannot win immediately many people give up and go out of the sport almost before they have begun. This is not the right approach. There is much to learn but only by being willing to learn and by persevering can one possibly hope to attain the success that one might yearn for. This particularly applies to breeders of the trimmed breeds; but even with the smooth-coated breeds, for top awards the dog must be in fit muscular condition with a gleaming coat and be happy in his job.

Of course it is true that some people have the ability to handle a dog and to prepare a dog much better than others. They seem to do it naturally and this is bound to be upsetting for those who do not take to it quite so easily and do not have the same excellent rapport with their animals. Practice will make perfect, so do not give up: just go on learning, watching and practising and your dedication will be rewarded.

Before considering in detail the show preparation and presentation of your dog, it is worth bringing to your attention the Kennel Club's Rules and Regulations for the preparation of dogs for exhibition. If a dog is exhibited at a show after having been prepared in contravention of any of the Regulations the owner of that dog and any person who

73

prepared the dog for exhibition or assisted in such preparation in any way or who handled the dog at the show or assisted in the handling in any way renders himself liable to disciplinary action under Kennel Club Rules and Regulations. A dog that is exhibited in a condition which contravenes the Regulations shall be disqualified from winning any award made to it at that show.

The Kennel Club (this applies equally to the American Kennel Club) may without previous notice order the examination of any dog at any show. It is therefore of the utmost importance that you adhere to the rules and here they are (the American Kennel Club rules are essentially the same).

1. No dyeing, colouring, tinting, darkening, bleaching or other matter may be used to alter or improve the markings of a dog. Dry white chalk may be used for cleaning provided that it is removed from the coat before the dog enters the ring. No coloured powder may be applied to the coat of a dog either before or at a show.

2. No cutting, piercing, breaking by force or any kind of operation or act which destroys the tissue of the ears or alters the natural formation of a dog or any part thereof may be practised and nothing may be done calculated in the opinion of the General Committee to deceive except operations certified to the satisfaction of the General Committee to be necessary. (These are the removal of dew claws and the shortening of tails as required in the official standards for certain breeds—see page 147.)

3. The setting of the teeth may not be artificially altered.

4. No oil, lacquer, greasy or sticky substance which has been used in the preparation of a dog for exhibition shall be allowed to remain in the coat of the dog at the time of exhibition.

These then, are the basic rules that you must obey in your preparation of your show dog. Many people find it difficult just to know where legitimate show preparation ends and where any form of disguise or faking begins. Many judges do not know either and when a clever fake is put in front of them they fail to recognise it. Any judge is faced with a very difficult decision even if he does recognise that the dog is not presented correctly. Does he report it as asked to do in the Kennel Club rules, or does he just pretend that he did not notice it, and simply fail to place the dog? This is certainly the line of least resistance, maybe not the right answer, but it is up to each judge to make up his own mind. The exhibitors soon know the reactions of the judges and some will show dogs that are maybe just slightly titivated, perhaps sprayed with

74

lacquer and not quite in accordance with the rules, but would not dream of showing them in this state under other judges. One must draw one's own conclusions.

In a book of this sort one can only speak generally about the presentation of your dog of your choice: you can then go on and consult the more specialized breed books. The essentials, however, apply to all dogs. The first essential for any dog is good feeding and exercising and if you wish to get your dog into top-class show condition you must feed the best possible diet that you can afford. I have always favoured raw meat or raw tripe plus a very good biscuit meal with raw eggs, milk and bone meal the only additions. This has proved very successful and with this diet I have never had any trouble in keeping show dogs in top class condition with healthy gleaming coats and bright eyes. If one does not feed properly one cannot expect the dog to look right; and as the breeders of yesterday used to say: what you do not put in you cannot get out.

Feeding must be regulated according to the size of the breed and also according to the amount of exercise that each individual dog takes. Exercise is vital to the show dog to keep him in good bloom and vigour. All breeds require daily walks on the pavements or hard surfaces to ensure that their muscles are kept in hard condition, that their toe nails are kept short, that their pasterns are not allowed to weaken and generally to keep their whole system in tip-top condition. Show dogs should never just be left to exercise in their own run. They will get bored with the same old surroundings and in any case all show dogs should be taken out to get used to traffic and all the noises that go with the world today outside the kennels. It is essential that the show dog is 'humanized' in this respect otherwise on arrival at the shows with all their strange noises he can be very easily upset.

The best time to introduce your show dog to the outside world is after he or she has finished his full course of injections and has already been trained to go happily on a collar and lead. Take him into the village or town and little by little introduce him to all the strange things that he might see or hear—children in prams, bicycles and the roar of traffic. The idea of having a radio in kennels is a very good one. This gets the dogs used to quite a variety of sounds and it allows them to accept these when they go to unfamiliar surroundings, i.e. the first show. There is so much that you can prepare your dog for and all this enables him to settle to the role of show dog much more quickly and easily. Have great patience with him when you are introducing him to these new scenes and noises, talk to him encouragingly and kindly, and give him plenty of praise if he is good. The dog will gain confidence in you, and as the dog's handler in the show ring you will have gone a long way towards making him want to please you and do as you ask. What a joy it is to handle such a dog, as so often with a little more training you can teach him to stand in a disciplined way on his own four legs, look up at you for the promise of a special little tit-bit, and freely show off his virtues.

All breeds require daily grooming and attention to skin. For the short-haired breeds all that is necessary is for a hound glove or a chamois leather to be taken over the coat at the same time as you inspect the skin for any unwelcome parasites. There are so many good preparations on the market today that will quickly get rid of these pests; if their presence is noticed straight away all to the good.

Ears must be checked regularly so that they can be kept in good condition. Smooth-coated breeds seldom suffer from ear problems but breeds with pendulous ears such as spaniels, setters and certain hounds can have their share of problems due to the fact that there is not so much circulation around the ears. Certain breeds such as poodles have hair growing inside their ears and this must be pulled out periodically. If this is not done and the hair continues to grow, wax and dirt will collect round the hair and shut off the air circulation causing infection. Ears can be easily kept clean by gently wiping a piece of cotton wool soaked in antiseptic around the ear. Never poke into the ear with anything that is hard as this could so easily damage it and cause the dog great pain and discomfort. If the ear is particularly dirty and your dog seems unhappy and keeps shaking his head from side to side seek professional advice straight away as without this help ear trouble can become quite chronic and very difficult to cure. Ears are very delicate; if they are not clean and are irritating the dog this will certainly tell on his performance in the ring. A sensitive ear can be held at a different angle from the other one; the lead may then catch the sore ear and the dog will try to scratch it off.

Eyes should be watched and kept clear of any stale mucus. Dogs that have their eyes more exposed than others particularly require watching as if mucus accumulates in the eye corners it can cause irritation and staining, which can spoil the look of a show dog.

In the course of daily grooming make regular checks of teeth and gums. This particularly applies to the older dogs when tartar or calculus collects and this can easily be removed with a scaling instrument as used by dentists. The instrument should be placed under the gum margin and with an upward or downward movement the tartar can be scraped away. Do take special care not to injure the gums and if the dog is difficult and obviously hates the idea of such an operation it is better to have it done by your Veterinary Surgeon who can give him a general anaesthetic. It is amazing in judging dogs how often one finds that care of the teeth seems to be a slightly neglected part of the dog's presentation and in many cases quite a lot of tartar is left on the teeth.

In the longer-coated breeds grooming is not quite so simple and apart from the attention to ears, teeth and toe nails, there is an art in the correct presentation of the coat.

Treatment of the coat, of course, varies according to the breed and the type of coat. When a good length of coat is desired the comb should be used very sparingly because if it is used erratically or without due care and attention, the coat will break and this is not what you want. A good stiff brush will keep the coat in good condition provided it is used every day and any tangles should be very carefully teased out with the aid of a little coat oil. I always feel that breeders specializing in these long-coated breeds—Afghans, Shih Tzus, Lhasa Apsos, Yorkshire Terriers, Pekinese—are a special breed themselves and I have nothing but admiration for the care and attention that goes into the presentation of these dogs for the show ring. Some owners are really masters of the art and if you want to learn how to do it have a chat with them. They are proud of their dogs and will be only too pleased to tell you their secrets, or some of them. However, do not approach them just before they go in to the show ring as they will be concentrating on their exhibit and trying to get that last little bit of hair into place. Wait till after they have exhibited their dogs and I am sure they will help you.

In breeds where the texture of the coat should be hard it is inadvisable to bath the dogs the day immediately before the show. This should be done some days before the show to allow the coat to regain its correct texture and for its natural oil to come back.

For those breeds that require trimming—and this particularly applies to a great many of the terrier breeds—many weeks of preparation are necessary to get the dog into show condition. Any of the trimmed terrier breeds such as the Norfolk, Norwich, Scottish Terrier, Wire Fox Terrier, West Highland White Terrier, etc. will become so shaggy if they are left untrimmed that the whole outline of the dog will be masked. When it is noticed that a new coat is coming through it is essential that the old coat be taken out completely. This is done by

77

hand: at no time should clippers be used. Clippers will make the dog's coat lose that coarse texture considered essential by those who prepare terriers for show and demanded by the standard of the breed. Plucking the old coat out by finger and thumb is the accepted method with perhaps the help of a stripping knife for some parts of the coat. This method allows the person stripping the coat very easily to shape the coat to enhance the dog's appearance.

In employing the finger-and-thumb method grasp the ends of the hair between your first two fingers and thumb so that small amounts of dead or unwanted hair can be pulled out very easily with a quick snapping action of your fingers. This will allow the new hair to grow in; depending on the breed, this usually takes about a month. Once the dog starts to come into full coat it is very important that the coat be checked every day to make sure that any dead coat is removed and to groom the furnishings.

In trimming any terrier breed and other breeds such as Schnauzers, Bouviers, etc. the whole idea is to emphasize the breed's distinctive characteristics. The Scottish Terrier should have a full beard and overhanging eyebrows. The West Highland White Terrier has no eyebrow definition but as with the Scottish Terrier the body coat presents a natural skirted appearance and so very little shaping of the legs is required. If you intend to prepare your own terriers for the show ring, take some lessons from those who are experienced in this art. It is a very special art and even learning just the rudiments of it from someone else rather than finding out by trial and error will save time and money; in preparing a terrier's coat for the show ring mistakes can mean months of not being able to show, as a new coat can take a very long time to come in.

Perhaps the art of trimming reaches a peak in the grooming and presentation of the three sizes of poodles. If you brush your poodle out well three or four times a week the fact that you have kept him well groomed will save a lot of time when you have to bath your dog before a show. Never at any time bath a dog that is matted. All tangles or matts must be brushed out *before* the dog is allowed into the water otherwise you will have a very difficult job to disentangle the matts when he comes out of his bath.

Start on the dog's hindquarters and brush upward and then downward in short quick strokes and make sure that you really get beneath the surface coat. Your hand should tell you whether there are any matts present and if there are, carefully free them. From the back legs go to the front legs and then on to the body coat working from back to front. Thereafter move on to the head and ears and make sure that you do not break any of the fringes. Having got your dog completely brushed out (and as he should be well acquainted with this procedure from puppyhood there should be no problems) the next step is to bath him. There are very many good shampoos on the market for this purpose but do make sure that you have everything to hand before you start the operation; chaos will reign if you think you can leave your dog in the bath while you go to get something you have forgotten.

Presumably you will be aiming to show your poodle in the Puppy Clip to begin with and from then on the Lion Clip and its many variations. Here again it is advisable that you should take some lessons on how to go about achieving the best results. Although you can learn much from the specialized books on this subject, there is nothing like practical experience to train your eye to the lines to follow in clipping out your poodle to whatever pattern you may wish. There are many good instructors and the professionals advertise in the dog magazines. If, of course, you have a friend who is prepared to teach you, all to the good, but make sure that your friend is well qualified in the art.

If you bought your foundation bitch from a reputable kennel it may well be that the kennel owners will be able to assist you, or at least supply you with the basic knowledge for you to improve on with experience.

Another breed where the coat receives rather special care is the Yorkshire Terrier. The texture, length and colour of the coat is one of the breed's most important show features and to safeguard the coat it must be tied up in ribbons. This has a slight disadvantage in that it tends to put a wave into the coat and the standard demands that it should be free of any wave. The coat therefore has to be brushed carefully to bring it back to its normal state.

There are many other dogs that require a general tidy up of the coat before entering the show ring. The Cocker Spaniel will need slight trimming at the feet, tail and top of the ears plus the removal of long, uneven hairs over the body generally. This should be done a few days before the show but if the coat is very heavy, work on it should be done several weeks before the show. This also applies to the other Spaniel breeds, with the exception of the Irish Water Spaniel whose coat requires rather more attention.

The German Shepherd Dog requires regular grooming to keep his coat in good condition with perhaps the finishing touches done with a good leather chamois or hound glove. There are many dogs in this category, and particularly the smooth-coated varieties; but care must be taken when the dog is casting his coat. The sooner the old coat is helped to come out the quicker the new will come in and this can be done by regular grooming with a good stiff brush or glove.

All serious grooming of show dogs should be done at home beforehand and not at the show where only a very quick touching up should be necessary. Apart from shortage of time at the show, there is the question of making as little mess at a show as possible. Venues these days are difficult for organizers to come by and due to the thoughtlessness of some exhibitors some of them have been lost to dog shows.

There is a great art in the presentation and preparation of our show dogs; you need to spend considerable time if you are to master it to the fullest degree and therefore give your dog his proper chance on the day of the show. If you are not prepared to dedicate yourself to this task then I would advise you to stay with the short-coated or smooth-coated dogs which do not require the time that the longer-coated varieties demand. These breeds will give you great pleasure without the need to cope with a coat that is difficult for you to manage and keep in the correct condition and so put you and your dog at a disadvantage in the show ring. Remember that it should be your pleasure to present your dog for the show ring and if you do not enjoy spending hours on grooming your dog then you would do better to concentrate on the many other breeds that will give you the same satisfaction with much less work.

As already mentioned it is important that show prospects should be trained to stand correctly from an early age, on a table if it is a breed that is judged on the table, and otherwise on the floor. It should be done only for a brief period each day until the youngster learns to recognize what is expected.

Depending on the breed and the accepted method of handling in the show ring practise regularly at home but never long enough to finish up with a bored dog. If you have never handled a dog in the ring before go to your local shows and watch what the judges expect of the exhibitors and how the exhibitors show your chosen breed. Although it is not always practised in many breeds it is so nice if you can teach your dog to show on a loose lead, that is, not strung up but with freedom to move his legs and body about. Some dogs are natural showgoers: they just love the whole experience and even appreciate the applause if they win the class. There is nothing better than to see a dog showing naturally at the end of a loose lead, and this undoubtedly enhances one's chances of being placed, tending to catch the judge's eye more than a heap of a dog being pulled and pushed into some sort of reluctant stance. Dogs have to be happy to show; there is, for example, nothing worse than a breed that should carry its tail in the upright position slinking along with it between its legs. Temperament in a show dog is of the utmost importance; we all know of the dog that shows so well at home but the minute he enters the ring simply does not want to know about it. I have had two of these and there is simply nothing you can do about it except leave them at home where they are happy.

Another problem is the dog that appreciates that his handler is nervous; the minute he enters the ring a certain something is transmitted down the lead from the handler and the dog, like his handler, finishes up a nervous wreck. If after a bit of practice at several shows this state of nervousness does not improve I would suggest that the handler try someone else at the end of the lead in the hope that they will not be so unsettled and be able to give the dog the confidence it needs.

Great patience is required with dogs that are not happy show dogs and for this sort of dog it is perhaps better to wait for the out-of-door shows where all the circumstances are much more natural.

There are many good training classes run by local canine societies that are most helpful to the newcomers to dog shows and I would recommend that anyone new to showing a dog should join one of these societies. Details of such societies can be obtained from the Kennel Club. At these classes the dog will be handled by a judge and expected to walk round the ring with other dogs and learn to do his own little stint on his own. This is excellent practice for both handler and dog and many very experienced handlers take their new stock to these classes for experience and to watch their reactions to the whole thing. An over-jubilant and bouncy dog can be taught to calm down and be examined by the judge without fuss. The same applies to the nervous dog and if he can just go to these classes and be handled by the judge, very sympathetically, once a week, if there is going to be an improvement in his temperament, this will do it. These classes are non-competitive and are specially held to help the novice exhibitor and the new puppy.

Never be short of praise for your dog when it has done as you have asked it. A little tit-bit should always be carried to give to him as a reward. There are many morsels now specially packed in little bags that dogs love and these can be used to help show your dog on a loose lead. By standing back from the dog and facing him four-square let him see that you have one of his special sweets or a piece of liver. Make him look up for it and without attracting any other exhibits' attention in the ring (this is a fault and could be objected to), give him one of his special treats; having eaten it he will look up for more. If these are kept in a pocket he will soon get to know just what is there and will learn to show quite naturally.

Dogs are very fond of liver and I find it best to make it quite hard by over-cooking it in the oven or under the grill. When it is cool, pieces should break away easily thus making it easier to handle; the dogs seem to love it like this and when they will not respond to other things they will generally clamour for their liver.

Of course there are dogs that will not make the most of themselves and in such cases you have no option but to get down to them and try to make them look good posed. When you stand them up make sure that their legs are correctly placed, both the front and rear. Make the dog hold his head up, and try to make sure that his back is level, if this is what the standard demands. Practice at home is of the utmost importance and is usually well rewarded with good presentation in the show ring.

I feel it is unwise to take your show dog to Obedience Training as the training offered here is quite different from what is required in the show ring. For instance an obedience-trained dog is required to sit and stay. At no time do you wish to make your show dog sit except when he is either waiting to be seen by the judge or after being judged. Ringcraft training classes are much more useful to both dog and handler and can be of immense help in giving experience to young dogs and new handlers.

9

Kennel Clubs throughout the world

Most countries have their own Kennel Club, to control the showing and breeding of dogs, although systems vary somewhat throughout the world.

The Fédération Cynologique Internationale controls every aspect of breeding and showing in all European and South American Countries except Britain. The FCI, as it is known, was founded on 22 May 1911, the original participants being Germany, Austria, Belgium and Holland. The President, Vice President and the members of the sub-committees are elected annually, the General Secretary, the Treasurer and the three technical members every three years. The Annual General Meeting is held in the country of the acting President.

There are two major types of FCI shows: firstly the CACIB Show where International Certificates are awarded and secondly the CAC Show where the National Certificates are awarded.

GREAT BRITAIN

The Kennel Club was formed in 1873 by Mr Sewallis Evelyn Shirley of Ettington. In these days it was housed in a small flat of three rooms only at 2, Albert Mansions, Victoria Street, London. The Club remained there until May 1877 when it moved to 29A Pall Mall, London. The Kennel Club is now established at 1–4, Clarges Street, London.

Trustees of the Kennel Club were first appointed in 1877 and the *Kennel Gazette* was founded in 1880; and in that year a system of registration of dogs was adopted.

It is perhaps amusing to note that in 1903 it was reported that the Committee work was exceptionally heavy and that during that year 341 licences to hold shows were granted. Today licences for about 4,000 shows per year are issued with the consequent tremendous work involved for both Committees and Kennel Club Staff.

From these small beginnings the Kennel Club progressed steadily onwards and in 1973 celebrated its Centenary Year. On 28 March of that year the Club was honoured by a visit from its Patron, Her Majesty the Queen, herself a very dedicated and distinguished breeder of dogs. A banquet was held in the Guildhall on the 2 May 1973, to celebrate the Centenary of the Club and guests from 21 overseas Kennel Clubs attended this great function—over 630 people were present.

Throughout the Centenary Year much thought was given to the revision of the Constitution of the Kennel Club and the amended Constitution came into effect on 1 January 1974.

The controlling Committee of the Kennel Club is the General Committee and it was not until 1979 that ladies were elected to this Committee. This is the senior committee, with authority over all others and consists of 24 members to include the Chairman and Vice Chairman. Eight members come up for re-election every third year.

The Disciplinary Committee, House Committee, Finance & General Purposes Committee and Stud Book and Registration Sub-Committee all come directly under the General Committee. The Executive Committee comes next in seniority to the General Committee and this in its turn controls the Show Regulations Committee, Judges Sub-Committee, Breed Standards Sub-Committee and the Working Trials and Obedience Committee.

The objects of the Kennel Club are as follows:

The Kennel Club exists mainly for the purpose of promoting the improvement of Dogs, Dog Shows, Field Trials, Working Trials and Obedience Tests and its objects include the classification of breeds, the Registration of Pedigrees, Transfers, etc., the Licensing of Shows, the framing and enforcing of Kennel Club Rules, the awarding of Challenge, Champion and other Certificates, the Registration of Associations, Clubs and Societies and the publication of an Annual Stud Book and a monthly Kennel Gazette.

Every year about 4000 dog shows and matches are held, plus approximately 300 Field and Working Trials. All these shows, matches and trials come under the jurisdiction of the Kennel Club. The shows vary widely from Exemption Shows run in conjunction with a village fête or charity organization to the very large Championship Shows, the best known of these being Cruft's, the Kennel Club's own show (see page 106).

At the end of 1982 there were 26 General Championship Shows including Cruft's, 11 Group Championship Shows and 452 Breed Club Shows. These Breed Club shows were allocated as follows: Hounds, 79; Gundogs, 77; Terriers, 59; Utility, 59; Working, 118; Toys, 60.

The breeds included in the above Groups are listed in an Appendix, page 141.

Among the breeds listed in the Appendix you will see some marked with an asterisk (*). These breeds have not yet qualified for Challenge Certificates—they have not gained enough representations at the Kennel Club and a good enough representation at the shows. At the end of 1982 there were 125 breeds with the right to gain Challenge Certificates, and it had already been announced that in 1984 Belgian Shepherd Dogs (Tervuerens) were to be granted Challenge Certificates, and no doubt their supporters were delighted.

So much for the awarding of Challenge Certificates, but many breeders are equally pleased when their young stock wins a Kennel Club Junior Warrant. To qualify for this the dog must obtain 25 points while eligible to compete as a Junior, i.e. under 18 months of age. The scale of points is as follows:

1. For each first prize in a Breed Class at a Championship Show where Challenge Certificates were offered for the Breed, three points.

2. For each first prize in a Breed Class at a Championship Show where Challenge Certificates were not offered for the Breed, or at an Open Show, one point.

A class open to more than one variety of a breed is not a Breed Class. Only registered owners at time of qualification may apply. Application forms for a Junior Warrant must be obtained from the Kennel Club.

At the end of 1981 the registrations applied for by the breeder totalled 100,130 which was a decrease of 14 per cent on 1980. There were 73,016 registrations made other than by the breeder and this gave a total of 173,146. There were 58,084 Transfers and 7,349 Export Pedigrees. One can readily appreciate the tremendous volume of work that is carried out by the Registration Department and it is obvious that the introduction of a computer has helped in its efficient running.

The Show Department of the Kennel Club is also very heavily loaded and with approximately 1,600 Registered Societies all permitted to organize three shows in one year if they so wish there is a very heavy demand on this department. Some feel that there are too many shows and that the number could be cut to two per Society but as long as entries continue to prove financially able to support the Society, the

Committees concerned are reluctant to cut down on any of their shows. Some Societies, of course, do not take their full quota of shows and this particularly applies to those Societies that run the large General Championship Shows.

Before a Society can have permission to run a show at all it must be registered with the Kennel Club and pay an annual Maintenance of Title fee and abide by the Rules and Regulations set down by the Kennel Club.

The Kennel Club has a reciprocal agreement with the following countries: Australia, Barbados, Belgium, Bermuda, Brazil, Burma, Canada, Caribbean, Chile, Colombia, Denmark, East Africa, Finland, France, Germany, Guernsey, Holland, Hong Kong, India, Ireland, Italy, Jamaica, Jersey, Malaysia, Malta G.C., Monaco, New Zealand, Norway, Pakistan, Portugal, Singapore, South Africa, Spain, Sweden, Switzerland, Uruguay, and U.S.A.

At the two World Conferences of Kennel Clubs, one organized by the Kennel Club in London in 1978 and the other organized by the Scottish Kennel Club in 1981 to celebrate their Centenary year, great stress was put on the Standardization of the Breed Standards. It is hoped that the Kennel Club will work towards this ideal and it was voted by the countries present at the Scottish Conference that the Kennel Club should be instructed to try to make progress both by correspondence and personal contact. This standardization of the breed standards would go a long way in helping judges from all countries in the world who encounter the slight differences in the standards that at present exist. Let us all hope that we may have some conclusive decisions at an early date.

There is housed at Clarges Street a magnificent library to which members have access. On guard outside the premises stands the Kennel Club Hound. The original of this Foxhound was cast in 1925 from a sculpture by Captain Adrian Jones and modelled on a hound from the Old Berkeley Pack. The Hound was presented to the Kennel Club in 1928 and although he may never have hunted the Berkeley county he is known to all the visitors that have passed through the doors of the Kennel Club.

The Club has approximately 600 Members of both sexes who have to be proposed and seconded by an existing member and approved by the respective committees. Luncheon is available in the Club from Monday to Friday and members may entertain their guests.

Like all governing bodies the Kennel Club has its critics. It has

A dam and her litter; note the overhead lamp

Last-minute preparation at the show. All major grooming should be done at home

YEO BRO
M
BRISTOL

A Sealyham being
prepared by a professional
handler in the USA

Cutting nails

served dogdom very well for over 100 years and we must certainly hope it will continue to do so. It has grown out of all proportion since its early days and it is difficult to keep abreast of this tremendous increase.

Committee members give their time in an honorary capacity and one sometimes wonders if those who proffer criticism of the Kennel Club fully appreciate how much free time members of the various Committees devote to the dog world.

THE UNITED STATES AND CANADA

The American Kennel Club was founded in 1884 and now has its headquarters at 51 Madison Avenue, New York. The first registered dog in the AKC was the English Setter, Adonis. The AKC does not have individual memberships. It is composed of more than 375 autonomous dog clubs throughout the United States. Each club exercises its voting power through a representative known as a delegate. These delegates are the legislative body of the AKC making the rules and electing directors from their number.

The AKC takes about a million new registrations each year and licenses about 1,000 Championship Shows, where points can be won to make a dog a Champion. Some 6,000 dogs gain their titles each year, very considerably more than in any other country in the world.

To become an American Champion a dog must win 15 Championship points, but this total must include two Majors. A Major is a show with the rating of three, four or five points and these must be won under two different judges. The final points are based on the number of dogs and bitches which are exhibited at a particular show. Every show catalogue must have the schedule of points printed in full. Five is the highest number of points that can be won and one is the lowest.

In America professional handlers are more the rule than the exception and the standard of handling and presentation is very high indeed. With this professional approach I have always found it a very great pleasure to judge in America apart altogether from the great satisfaction in judging good dogs.

In America one is not allowed to judge more than 175 dogs in one day. If there are more than this number some of the dogs will be taken away and given to another judge. This is not entirely satisfactory as naturally an exhibitor often comes for a particular judge's opinion. However, no critiques are called for in America either during the judging or afterwards and this certainly eases one's task considerably.

The American Kennel Club are justly proud to own one of the finest reference libraries of dog books in the world. This library houses more than 10,000 volumes and included in this collection are famous prints and oil paintings by the old masters as well as modern artists. Also included are photographs for the study of every known breed of dog.

It is interesting to note that the American Kennel Club have decided that their Working Group is rather unmanageable as it is, and have decided to split it into two, with effect at 1 January 1983. Eighteen breeds remain in the Working Group, and 14 in the new Herding Group. Details are given in the Appendix, page 149. The AKC has further announced that if it is later decided by the board of the AKC that the interests of a breed in the Working Group would be better served by being reassigned to the Herding Group, then a change will be made.

The Centenary of the American Kennel Club falls in 1984; in honour of the occasion it is planned, at the time of writing, to hold a World Congress in Philadelphia in November of that year.

The Canadian Kennel Club was founded in September 1888 at London, Ontario and once again an English Setter was the first dog to be registered.

The shows in Canada are run on similar lines to those of the American Kennel Club but in Canada a judge can withhold winner's points if he or she does not consider that the standard of the animal is high enough to warrant points. This is similar to the system in Great Britain where a judge is quite entitled to withhold a Challenge Certificate.

The points system in Canada is just slightly different from that in the USA, and a little lower. A dog or bitch requires 10 points in Canada to become a Champion and this does not vary with the sex. A dog must get his points under three different judges and must defeat at least one of his own breed in so doing or be placed in his group with five or more competing breeds.

Canada and the USA recognize one another's registrations and this makes it quite easy for dogs registered in one country to be shown in the other.

AUSTRALIA AND NEW ZEALAND

Australia and New Zealand follow a pattern similar to the British method of judging and the breed standards adopted in these two countries are those approved by the Kennel Club in London, plus, of course, local standards for Australian breeds such as the Australian Cattle Dog and the Australian Kelpie.

The Australian National Kennel Council was formed by mutual agreement of eight canine administrative bodies. These organizations represented each of the six States and the two Federal Territories. Each State holds dog shows regularly but the highlight of each state is the annual Royal Agricultural Show which attracts very big entries and it is the usual practice to engage overseas judges for these major events. I was privileged to judge the Sydney Royal in 1980 and although it was a marathon task of judging something in the region of 300 dogs for ten days it was a most pleasurable one and a very memorable one.

The New Zealand Kennel Club was founded in 1886 with the Governor of New Zealand, Sir William Jervois, as its patron. The first Championship Shows were held in the early 1920's. Shows in New Zealand are very similar to those in Australia and the Groups are only slightly different from those in Britain and Australia.

SCANDINAVIA

The Scandinavian countries, which are strongholds in many breeds, come under the jurisdiction of the FCI but they have their own Scandinavian Kennel Union which was founded in 1953 to co-ordinate the canine activities in Finland, Denmark, Norway and Sweden. The Swedish and Finnish Kennel Clubs were founded in 1889, the Danish Kennel Club in 1897 and the Norwegian Kennel Club in 1898.

In all Scandinavian countries a critique is written by the judge on each and every dog at the time of judging. These critiques are given to the exhibitors on the completion of judging. Naturally, this takes much more time to complete and the judge is not permitted to judge more than 75 dogs on any one day. This is the rule but I have to admit that I have known this number stretch quite considerably on occasions!

SINGAPORE AND MALAYSIA

The Singapore Kennel Club was founded in September 1972 as a result of a dichotomy of the then Malaysia-Singapore Kennel Association into two separate autonomous bodies, the other being the Malaysian Kennel Association. Before that date control of canine matters of both territories was undertaken by the Malayan Kennel Association which was incorporated in August 1925. Dog shows were held in Malaysia, mainly Kuala Lumpur, and in Singapore under Show Rules formulated by the MKA and patterned on those of the Kennel Club, London, with which the MKA was affiliated. The first Championship Show was held in October 1964 in Kuala Lumpur and Singapore exhibitors came across the causeway with their dogs. This free movement of dogs across the causeway continued until 1970 when there was a serious outbreak of rabies in Northern Malaysia and the Singapore Government placed a total ban on the entry of dogs from Malaysia. This made it impossible to hold joint Championship Shows and in September 1972 the MSKA dissolved to be replaced by the Singapore Kennel Club and the Malaysian Kennel Association.

Many good dogs have been imported into these two countries and it is very pleasing to note the continual improvement in their own home-bred stock.

SOUTH AFRICA

The Kennel Union of South Africa was formed in 1891 and the Headquarters of the controlling body was established in Cape Town. During most of the history of the Union it has had affiliated clubs in Zimbabwe and Zambia and at the present time the number of affiliated clubs subject to its jurisdiction is approximately 150.

Wherever there is a Kennel Club there are dog shows. Dog shows require judges and judges travel from all corners of the world to officiate at these shows. On each and every occasion they are accorded the greatest hospitality and courtesy and we can only hope that they, in their turn, give graciously the value of their knowledge and experience and in so doing help improve the quality of dogs throughout the globe.

10

The history of dog shows

How did the idea of a dog show come about? Research does not give any positive answer to this question but perhaps it originated from some of the sports of by-gone days such as bull-baiting, dog-fighting and bear-baiting. The first public livestock show in the world was held in Sussex in 1798 and the Country Fair was making itself known in many parts of England.

It was, however, not until 28 and 29 June, 1859 that the first dog show was held with the venue the Town Hall, Newcastle on Tyne. It was advertised to the public in *The Field*, 28 May 1859. Official entries were taken, a catalogue published, official judges were appointed and they made official results. Dog authorities throughout the world recognize this event as the world's first ever dog show. It was organized by Messrs Shorthose and Pape at the suggestion of Mr R. Brailsford. The exhibits were confined to Pointers and Setters and there were 60 entries and three judges appointed for each breed. Mr Jobling, Mr Robson and Mr J. H. Walsh judged the classes for Pointers and Mr Foulger, Mr Brailsford and Mr J. H. Walsh judged those for Setters. It is interesting to note that at this particular show one of the judges for Setters took the first prize in Pointers while one of the judges of the Pointer Classes took first prize in Setters. This could not now happen under today's Kennel Club Rules as no judge is allowed to show on the same day as he or she judges.

The prizes at this first show were guns from Mr Pape's factory and these double-barrelled guns were worth then about £15–£20.

I quote from an old copy of *Our Dogs*:

The show being a success, it induced Mr. Richard Brailsford, Mr. Frederick Burdett, Viscount Curzon (afterwards Earl Howe) and J. H. Walsh (Stonehenge) to organize a similar show of Sporting Dogs in Birmingham at the end of the same year (1859). This led to the formation of the present Birmingham Dog Show Society which has held a show in the Midland Metropolis every year since that date.

The Birmingham Dog Show Society is still going strong and is the oldest dog show in the world. From these small beginnings in 1859 Birmingham National had in 1982 the wonderful total of 17,064 entries made by 11,372 dogs. This show has Challenge Certificates for every breed and about 80 judges officiating over the three days of the show.

Shows continued to be held from 1859 onwards but there was no governing body, no rules or regulations and it was not until April 1873 that the world's first Kennel Club was formed in London. Mr Sewallis Evelyn Shirley of Ettington was the brain behind it. It was felt, even in those days, that with the increase of shows some official body should be in power to control a sport that was very rapidly growing and becoming just a little out of hand. If this seed of establishing a Kennel Club in these far off days had not been sown I hate to think what sort of mess our dog fancy would have been in today.

America held its first dog show in 1874. It was 10 years later that the American Kennel Club was formed, on 17 September, 1884.

The first Field Trial took place on Tuesday 18 April 1865 at Southill, Bedfordshire, over the estate of Mr Samuel Whitbred, M.P. The order of procedure at this early trial was similar to that which exists today.

In 1870 Mr Shirley and Mr Murchison agreed to run a show at the Crystal Palace, London. The Secretary was Mr G. Nutt and this show was a financial disaster, but the committee decided to go on with another show and in this case the loss was much less than that of the previous year.

The meetings for these Crystal Palace Shows took place at the British Hotel in Cockspur Street, an old-fashioned 'pub' that no longer exists. It was indeed the near impossible task of trying to organize these shows without a permanent Secretary, any staff or even a permanent office, far less the necessary money, that prompted Mr Shirley to found the Kennel Club. He became the Kennel Club's first Chairman and he held this appointment from 1873 until 1899 when he became the first President. This is a position that he held until his sudden death in 1904.

The Kennel Club's first show took place at Crystal Palace, Sydenham, on 17–20 June 1873. There were 975 entries and when one considers that the show ran over four days it must have been a very leisurely and pleasurable affair, in sharp contrast to the hustle and bustle of our shows today. The Show Manager was Mr Douglas, the Secretary Mr Roue and the Chairman Mr Shirley.

The Kennel Club ceased from 1882 to recognize any shows in Britain that were not held under their jurisdiction. In that year there were 28 shows held, ten years later there were 57 shows organized and at the turn of the century it had dropped slightly to 48 shows. Today we have over 4,000.

The Rev G. F. Hodson, a very popular and knowledgeable judge of these early days, reckoned that he travelled in his judging capacity about 10,000 miles per annum. I wonder what he would have thought of our 'jet-set' of today who think nothing of travelling to Australia one week, on to California the next and perhaps a Scandinavian tour the week after. Our regular judges travel very many hundreds of thousands of miles during any one year to judge dogs and no matter what land they visit there is always a warm welcome from humans and their canine friends.

The first Manchester Dog Show was held at the Belle Vue Zoological Gardens in 1861. Manchester still hold their Championship Show at this venue and in spite of many rumours that this old hall is to be rebuilt it still houses the Northern Classic. In 1862 there was a show at the New Agricultural Hall, Islington, London, and this show lasted for five days. There were 803 entries and it is interesting to note some of the breed entries. Mastiffs had 39 dogs, Newfoundlands had 26 in one class while on the other end of the line Irish Setters had 8 dogs entered and Beagles 15. Irish Setters can happily total between 300 and 400 dogs at our shows today and Beagles over 100.

The non-classified part of this Islington Show appeared to be the excitement of the day as it had no less than 54 dogs entered. The winner of this class seemed to be an Egyptian dog called Egil and those closely behind were described as Chinese dogs called Wong, Chin Chin and Chow Chow.

At this same venue in 1863 the first International Dog Show was held, and produced an entry of 1,678 dogs; but reports have it that there were about 2,000 dogs in the hall! The Secretary was a Mr S. Sidney, a personality very well known in connection with horse shows.

In 1863 on 30 November and 1–3 December, the fourth Birmingham Show was again held at the Old Wharf, Broad Street, with 570 entries. The largest division was the Sporting Group with Foxhounds at the top of the table. It is sad that we never see this lovely breed being shown at Kennel Club shows today. They are, of course, on display at the Masters of Harriers and Foxhounds' own shows throughout the country.

The first Scottish National Exhibition of sporting and other dogs was held on 20–22 February 1871, at the Burnbank Drill Hall, Glasgow and it had an entry of 383. This obviously stirred the Edinburgh dog fanciers and in the same year they organized the first Scottish Metropolitan Exhibition of Sporting and Fancy dogs in the Royal Gymnasium, Royal Crescent Park, Edinburgh. The entry was 789— double that received in Glasgow. There were fourteen judges, all male, and it was said that they had been imported from over the border. It is most pleasing to know that the Scots still continue this practice.

The Irish obviously became aware of dog shows about this time and on 18–20 January 1872 Dublin organized the Grand National Dog Show. This was held in the Exhibition Palace, Dublin and there were 365 entries.

On 24–25 June 1875, the first annual exhibition of Sporting and Fancy Dogs was held in the Ulster Hall, Belfast. There was an entry of 639 and there seemed to be only three judges for this event.

Kennel Club Rules and Regulations have changed very little over the years. In April 1973 the Kennel Club sanctioned Sunday Shows. There were mixed feelings about this innovation. Some felt that they wanted to have a Sunday at home to catch up with the many tasks that seem to collect in kennels. It was a day that so many judges set aside to write their reports or breed notes for the dog press. Indeed it was a day when so many of us found time to look and study our own dogs instead of judging others. These Sunday shows were very well supported and still are although some breeders might have hoped for the reverse!

The year 1975 saw the first Championship Show to offer no prize money. Here again was a very controversial move, but the idea has certainly caught on, and by far the majority of Championship Shows today have followed suit. It certainly has not affected the entry of these shows but it has helped to keep entry fees down to a sensible size.

Modern shows are much more lenient with exhibitors as to times they may arrive at the show and depart. Until the last few years it was quite usual for exhibitors to be at a show by 11 a.m. and with a special 'early removal' leave the show about 4 p.m., otherwise not until 6 p.m. Exhibitors do appreciate being allowed to arrive in time for their judging and once it is finished to be able to depart. Gone are the days of big kennels with staff to look after the dogs when the owners are away at a show and exhibitors who have to rush back to their kennels to look after their dogs are glad to have the extra hours spent at home.

Shows have grown and multiplied, and today the dog show world is full of activity from January to December. The summer months are crowded with outside shows, usually under a mass of canvas, and in the winter months halls are filled to capacity with dogs and their owners. One could attend a dog show in Britain twice or three times every week if one wished to do so and the dog shows are still developing.

WESTMINSTER DOG SHOW—AMERICA

The first Westminster Kennel Club show was held in New York at Gilmore's Gardens on 8–11 May 1877 with 1177 dogs entered. Since that date the show has been held annually—it is the oldest annual event of its kind in the United States.

The beginnings of Westminster originated in the bar of the Westminster Hotel where a group of sportsmen met periodically. They formed a club and built a training kennel to train and hunt their dogs. They hired a trainer and imported some dogs from England to use with their locally bred dogs. This Club was named Westminster after the hotel which, unfortunately, no longer exists. A Mr William Tileston was Chairman of the first show and Charles Lincoln was the Superintendent for the first six years.

The 1880 show was held at the original Madison Square Garden, New York. Except in a very few years, this show has been held in either the first or the two succeeding Madison Square Gardens, and for this reason American and Canadian dog fanciers like to think of the show as 'the Garden Show'. It is a 'Garden Show' to this day with lovely floral decorations tastefully executed.

The largest entry of this show came in 1937 when there were 3,146 dogs making 3,629 entries. This proved a problem for the organizers due to lack of space and it forced the show to limit entries—the 2,500th entry to arrive through the mail had to be the last—not altogether a satisfactory method of controlling entries.

The present Madison Square Garden is slightly smaller than either of the old Gardens and in 1970 the show started a new system, limiting entries to 3,000 over two days. Three groups of dogs were benched on one day and the other three groups on the next day. It is calculated that normally about 40 per cent of Westminster entries are Champions.

Westminster is the American Kennel Club's own show, just as Cruft's belongs to the English Kennel Club. Both these shows have restricted entries and consequently they are not the biggest shows in their respective countries. In 1982 for example, Westminster, while always the nation's prestige show, was for the first time not in the first 20 shows reckoned on entry numbers.

Westminster nowadays is held every February in New York and the presentation at this show is of the highest quality. It is the 'show of shows' in America and there is no question at all that full justice is done to the many great dogs that parade on its carpeted rings. It is right to call it a beautiful show with silver stainless steel, scarlet-roped stanchions dividing the rings that are always tastefully decorated with flowers. Anyone interested in dogdom should certainly try to visit at least once.

The final Groups and Best in Show are judged in the evening, the dogs are presented and shown in magnificent coats, gleaming with condition, and the judges, stewards and handlers add great lustre to the whole occasion by appearing in evening wear. It is a great occasion and everyone does their best to make it so.

11

Dog shows today

TYPES OF SHOWS IN GREAT BRITAIN

All shows in the UK come under the jurisdiction of the Kennel Club, whose Rules and Regulations must be adhered to. All dogs entered at Kennel Club shows must be registered at the Kennel Club, the only exception being the non-pedigree classes allowed at Exemption Shows.

At the bottom of the ladder in shows we have the *Exemption Show*; as the title implies, dogs not registered with the Kennel Club may compete. Permission to hold an Exemption Show must be granted by the Kennel Club, and may be given where there are not more than four classes for pedigree dogs. Such an event is normally held in conjunction with a local fête, gala or some charity happening. Registered canine societies and dog training clubs may not hold Exemption Shows. The classes (up to four) for pedigree dogs at Exemption Shows must be confined to any of the following: Any Variety Sporting Dog, Any Variety Hound, Any Variety Gundog, Any Variety Terrier, Any Variety Non Sporting Dog, Any Variety Utility, Any Variety Working, Any Variety Toy, Any Variety Puppy, Any Variety Open or any combination of the above groups. So that these shows be kept in the right mood, no dog is elegible for entry in the pedigree classes at an Exemption Show that has won a Challenge Certificate, has obtained any award that counts towards the title of Champion, or has attained the title of Champion. Very often the organizers schedule a Champions' parade, which is always very popular.

Over and above the four Kennel Club Classes the organizers may include further classes which may include such frivolous themes as: handler most like his or her dog, best fancy dress combination, the dog with the tail that wags most, the dog (or perhaps even owner) that the judge would like to take home. Such classes offer great variety; a very popular one is for the best child handler and dog.

As you will appreciate these Exemption Shows can be a marvellous day out for the whole family and their pet dog whether it is registered or not, and so often it is all in a very good cause, for example some deserving charity.

Next up the list come the *Sanction Shows*: these are restricted to Members of the Club organizing the show. No class higher than Post Graduate may be offered at a Sanction Show and this makes such shows ideal events for puppies and for new handlers. No dog that has won anything towards the title of Champion is allowed to compete, a rule which also applies to *Limited Shows* which are either for Members or limited to a specific area.

Open Shows are, as they suggest, open to all exhibitors and dogs. Open Shows can be benched or not but if there are more than a certain number of classes the Kennel Club insist that they are benched.

Breed Club Shows are shows confined to one breed and can be Limited, Open or Championship Show events.

Championship Shows are open to all unless the Society organizing the show have stipulated any restrictions, as Cruft's do, to control their entry. The only difference between Championship Shows and Open Shows is the fact that Kennel Club Challenge Certificates are on offer at the former; judges awarding them must be approved by the Kennel Club, and they must not have given Challenge Certificates in the same breed within the previous nine months. These Certificates are very eagerly sought by breeders and exhibitors: three Challenge Certificates under three different judges entitles a dog or bitch to have the title of Champion added to its name, provided that one of the Certificates is awarded after the dog is out of puppy. If not it is necessary for the puppy to collect a further Challenge Certificate after it becomes twelve months of age to qualify for the title of Champion.

Challenge Certificates, or C.C.'s as they are commonly called, are not easily gained in Britain and the cost of making a Champion in time, energy and money can be very substantial; it can be rather frustrating on occasions.

Championship Shows can either be General Shows with all breeds competing, Group Shows for dogs that come within the particular Group, i.e. Toys, Terriers, Working, Utility, Gundogs or Hounds, or Specialist Club Shows—only one breed. All Championship Show judges must be approved by the Kennel Club: everyone would probably agree that the approval or non-approval of Championship Show judges is one of the most controversial subjects in the dog game.

All General and Group Championship Shows must be benched but some of the breed shows with a smaller number of entries are permitted to be held without benching.

Some shows are run in conjunction with agricultural shows but these dog shows must still come under the jurisdiction of the Kennel Club. It is usual for such agricultural shows to have their own Dog Show Committee who take care of this section. These events can be of great interest to a family interested in livestock, and make a wonderful day out with dogs, horses, ponies, poultry, rabbits, cage birds, cattle etc. They are held during the summer months and if the weather is kind they certainly have a lot to offer.

The various types of classes at a show are always given in the schedule; these schedules are available from the Secretary of the show. Details are advertised in the dog press, i.e. *Dog World* and *Our Dogs*. Enclosed with the schedule you will find the entry form, and it is very important that you fill in this entry form very accurately. The entry form is the contract between yourself and the show society and if not correctly filled in it could mean the disqualification of your exhibit on the day of the show. When it is completed make quite sure that the form is posted to comply with the closing date for entries, and last but by no means least see that you have put in the right money, either cash, postal order or cheque.

After having done all that you can sit back and wait for the day of the show itself.

DOG SHOWS IN AMERICA

Shows throughout the world are run very much on the same lines as those in the UK. In America very few shows are benched, and the responsibility for the organization falls on professionals known as Show Superintendants. They work for professional companies which attend to show entries, lay-out, catering, benching (where appropriate), tentage etc. The Show Committee is responsible for the invitations to the judges. American shows are run very meticulously with regard to timing. After each breed a judge is required to note down the time started and the time finished. Personally I consider this a very good system, as it prevents judges from taking too long or too short a time over their entry.

In North America there are classes specially for Champions. Champions are not allowed to enter the Open Classes. Winners of First Place in Dog and Bitch Classes are eligible to compete for Winner's

Dog and Winner's Bitch—that is, at Championship Shows. Winner's Dog and Winner's Bitch are each awarded points, determined by the number of dogs competing according to the AKC Points Schedule. The second best dog or bitch is then chosen as a Reserve Winner, but gains no points. The Best of Breed Classes contain both male and female Champions, plus Winner's Dog and Winner's Bitch. A Best of Breed or Variety award qualifies a dog to represent its breed in its Group. As in the UK, the First Place winner in each of the Groups represents its Group for Best in Show. No matter which country and which system you are competing in, a Group win or—even better—a Best in Show win is a great achievement for owner, breeder and exhibitor, and just acclaim for a great dog.

WHAT HAPPENS AT A SHOW?

Shows are the stages on which exhibitors and breeders can show off their stock and compete against their fellow exhibitors, we hope in a good sporting manner. The details in the following account are based on shows in Britain, but shows throughout the world are essentially similar.

If you start at one of the smaller shows it is unlikely to be benched so that you will find the dogs sitting down where their owners have parked themselves, be it inside a hall or by the ringside at an out-of-door show. Most people today transport their dogs in crates in their cars and these crates are taken into the hall for the dog to use as his resting quarters throughout the show. Otherwise the dogs can be given a blanket or rug to settle down on beside their owners. Show dogs are really marvellous creatures as they do put up with a great deal of inconvenience: as long as they are with their owners they accept it all with great patience and fortitude.

A benched show is one where every dog is provided with a bench, and in accordance with Kennel Club Rules and Regulations dogs must be put on these benches except when they are being exercised or competing in the ring. At the back of the bench there is a large ring and the dog's benching lead, made of metal, is connected to the ring and the other end attached to his collar. This should be a leather collar and never a choke chain as quite obviously if the dog tried to get off the bench the choke chain would tighten with serious results. The benching for the toy breeds is in the form of a cage. This cage has a door at the front that fastens quite safely with a safety catch and the cage, made of wire, is a safe haven. The owners bring their own rugs or towels for the dogs to lie on and the show dogs soon learn that this is their own particular place for the duration of the show. Some dogs become quite possessive of this bench or cage and it is best not to try to touch them as they might resent a stranger intruding onto their property. Also their bench or cage is the place at a show where they can rest, and if they are continually disturbed it is very hard for them to give of their best when their turn comes to go into the ring.

At the smaller shows the judging ring can be surrounded by chairs or rope but at the larger benched events there can be up to 50 or 60 judging rings. The large Championship Shows are usually run over two or three days but one or two now extend to four and even five days. The same procedure applies from the smallest to the largest and they are all based on the same rules and regulations, set by the Kennel Club. The duration of a show depends on its size, but the General Championship Shows and the Open Shows usually start at about 10 a.m., and go on until about 6 p.m. If judges are overloaded with a breed it is common to start that breed at 9 a.m. If the schedule has said that judging will commence at 10 a.m., a common time for judging to start, it will start punctually at that time. We do have very large entries at our shows today, particularly at the Championship events, and it is essential that a strict timetable is adhered to. The Kennel Club prefer that a judge should not judge more than about 200 dogs at a Championship event but at Open Shows with the large variety classes there could be more like 400 dogs for one judge on one day. There is no greater training for judges than practical experience gained judging at the Limited and Open Shows throughout the land.

The judge will enter the ring with his or her judging book, obtained from the Secretary's Office. The judge will bear a badge signifying that he or she is the judge of the day. A steward or stewards, wearing their badges, will accompany the judge and it is the steward's task to muster the dogs into the ring at the correct time and for the correct class. All classes are numbered in the schedule and should be judged in schedule order. The stewards are supplied with a catalogue so that they may check that the correct dogs are entered in each particular class. It is not usual for a judge to have a catalogue but there is nothing in the Kennel Club Rules and Regulations that actually forbids it. It has not been unknown for a judge to have a quiet peep at a catalogue in some secluded spot perhaps just to make a note of a champion or two or to make sure whether a particular dog has been entered! I don't think this happens so much today as perhaps it once did!

The stewards will advise the judge when the class is ready to be judged and will, if requested by the judge, mark the absentees in the judging book. No alteration can be made to a judge's judging book except by the judge or with the judge's authority. As soon as the judge starts judging the stewards should retire to the corner of the ring where the judging table is situated. This, unfortunately, does not always happen but it is a Kennel Club Rule and should be obeyed. The stewards should in no way influence the judge but with a weak or unsure judge a dominating steward can exert a certain amount of influence. This should not be tolerated by the judge of the day. A judge is entitled to ask a steward to place the dogs that he has already judged in a previous class in the order that they were placed before and with the large entries that we have today this does save the judge valuable time particularly if he can rely on his stewards. Britain is one of the few countries that has repeat entries and judges coming from abroad do find this slightly confusing to begin with. These repeat dogs stand to one side until the judge has seen the new dogs in the class, and thereafter he may move them again or place them according to their merits.

Stewards at the shows do a marvellous job, all in an honorary capacity, and we would be lost without them. These people are dedicated to their job and although they are very happy to steward in most rings they do have their favourites—they get to know all the exhibitors in the particular breeds and this is most helpful.

When the judge has completed his class he will obey Kennel Club rules by placing the dogs, from left to right, down to fourth or fifth place. He will mark his book accordingly and thereafter the steward will present the winners with their prize cards, red for first, blue for second, yellow for third, green for fourth (or reserve, as it is often called), brown for fifth and usually white for any other cards that may be awarded. The dogs with their handlers then leave the ring. The stewards then call for the next class, and when all dogs are present, once again they will indicate this to the judge who will commence judging the new dogs. Again, the stewards will place the 'seen' dogs that have come into this class down one side of the ring if so requested by the judge.

Exhibitors and spectators who watch from the ringside can soon tell if the judge is in charge of the ring and competent for the job. The judge is not only judging but being judged and usually by a very critical

Championship Show Date

Breed Sex

Kennel Club Challenge Certificate

I am clearly of opinion that

owned by

(Name of Exhibit)

(Name of Owner)

is of such outstanding merit as to be worthy of the title of Champion.

(Signed)

(Judge)

KENNEL CLUB AWARD CARD FOR

BEST OF BREED

Breed Sex

Name of Exhibit

Signed

Judge

Kennel Club Challenge Certificate *(top)*   Kennel Club Best of Breed *(bottom)*

Old English Sheepdogs being shown
in America

Greyhounds being judged in a
Progeny Class in Britain

audience. A judge should try to look the part, and be dressed neatly, tidily, inconspicuously and with comfortable shoes. Judges should always arrive in good time so that they do not dash to the ring in a breathless state and look dishevelled before they start.

Most judges like to have a look at the dogs in a class and then ask them all to move round the ring in a circle. By doing this the judge should gain some idea of the quality of the class; very often one can pick one's winners from this first sight. Every individual dog is then handled by the judge either on the ground if it is one of the larger breeds or on a table if it is one of the smaller. Eyes, ears, mouth, teeth, overall balance of the head, neck, placement of shoulders, proportion of back and loin, quarters, tail, quality of coat—these are some of the points assessed by the judge. Thereafter the handlers will be asked to move the dogs one at a time. Some judges say straight up and down, others require a triangle and then up and down: by doing this the judge can see the dog move in profile when it is easier to assess his topline and smoothness of gait. Few breeds vary from this routine except perhaps the Alsatians or German Shepherd Dogs whose specialist judges require that they gait round and round and round the ring in some cases almost to the point of exhaustion of the handler and dog!

What are the judges looking for? You may well ask, as it sometimes appears even to the experienced eye at the side of the ring that there is no set pattern to the judge's final decisions. The Kennel Club Standards should be known to all judges, even the Limited Show judges, and these are the guidelines for the judges to apply. This is particularly important when the judge is judging at Championship level when Challenge Certificates are on offer.

By judging to a particular standard the judge must be able to recognize the type of animal that he is looking for, i.e. the particular shape of head, body, legs etc. that belong to that one breed. As well as type a judge must be able to see correct conformation, how the animal is constructed and when moved, just how he goes—for example, whether he moves close behind with his hocks nearly rubbing, a bit like a cow, or whether he spreads his hocks outwards to give a sort of spreading appearance. Correctly most dogs move with their hocks parallel to each other. In front most breeds are required to move quite straight with no inclination to cross in front or to paddle or weave. The Kennel Club Standards on each breed are quite definite on movement, and it is very important that these standards should be digested and retained in one's memory if a successful judging career is to be

103

established. One does not expect a Basset to move like a Terrier in front and nor does one expect a Chow to move like an Alsatian. These are very elementary facts that any judge should be well acquainted with before taking the centre of a dog judging ring. There is no doubt that the centre of the ring can be a very lonely place and once one is there one is quite alone but, we hope, equipped for that loneliness.

In judging it is important that one must be able to assess the whole animal and not just one single fault or one single virtue. It would make the life of a judge so much easier if having once found a fault the judge could discard the animal and not consider him further. It is sad that a few judges do tend to judge in this manner. In fact, the whole balance and type of the dog must be taken into consideration and then finally there is that elusive thing called 'quality' (see page 62). This is perhaps the most difficult thing to describe and for some it seems to be the most difficult thing to see. This is a pity because I feel that this thing called 'quality' is what makes a good dog an even better dog and so often a great one.

It is said that good judges must have the 'eye' to judge and that they are born and not made. This I am inclined to agree with: no matter what knowledge and experience a dog judge acquires, without an eye for a dog he or she will never make the top grade. With knowledge, experience and learning a judge can, of course, become reasonably efficient but the masters have an eye and this is the greatest asset to any judge. Top judges throughout the world have served a very long apprenticeship; even so the great majority of them would admit that they are still learning.

Apart from a judge's ability to assess the dogs it is absolutely essential that his integrity should be completely beyond question in every respect. It is no good a judge saying that if his friends show their dogs under him he is inclined to be harder on these dogs than on others. This is just as bad as giving his enemy's dog a better crack of the whip than the other exhibits. A judge must be completely impartial at all times and not only must justice be done it must be seen to be done.

Never ask a judge to tell you why he or she did not put you higher in the awards until after the judging is finished. Otherwise you could spoil the judge's concentration. Most of our judges are only too happy to tell exhibitors the reason for their placings on any particular dog and this particularly applies to newcomers to the dog game.

If you have been disappointed in a particular judge never forget that there is always another day with another judge: this hope for the future is what keeps us all going.

When a judge has finished all his classes in a particular breed the steward should call into the ring the unbeaten dogs who will compete for Best of Breed. At Open and Limited Shows the winner is given a Best of Breed Card and very often a rosette as well. At Championship Shows the procedure is a little more complicated. It is usual that after the dogs are judged unbeaten dogs will come back into the ring so that the judge can decide on the Best Dog and Reserve Best Dog. The top winning dog is then presented with the Kennel Club Challenge Certificate and the second best dog with the Reserve Challenge Certificate. If for any reason, the first dog is disqualified then the reserve winner will eventually get the Challenge Certificate. The same thing happens at the end of the bitch classes and a Challenge Certificate is awarded to the Best Bitch and Reserve to the second best bitch. The final is then decided between the Best Dog and Best Bitch and the winner of this is the Best of Breed. This dog or bitch then goes on for further competition in his own Group. A Beagle would go on to the Hound Group and a Miniature Poodle to the Utility Group. These Groups are not judged until all the breeds in the particular Group have finished judging. Group judging at the Championship Shows does not usually begin until about 4 p.m. and these Groups are judged by a judge who gives Challenge Certificates in several of the breeds in the Group. Some very experienced judges would be qualified to give Challenge Certificates in the great majority of the breeds in the Group if not all of them. The Kennel Club rules that a Group judge will not judge any of the individual breeds within that Group at that particular Show so that all the dogs that come to the Group judge are quite new to him or her on that day. This is surely fair.

After the completion of the Group judging the winner of the Group will stand by for the final Best in Show award. This is always a very exciting moment. As the majority of Championship Shows in Britain are held over more than one day it is essential for the Group winners on the first or second day to come back for this final competition. The Best in Show judge is an experienced judge and here again he or she is not allowed to judge a breed at that particular show. The Best in Show judge may judge all or any of the Groups at the show: perhaps the greatest job of all for any judge is to judge all Groups and Best in Show at a General Championship Show.

It is a great moment for any exhibitor and breeder to win Best in Show at any General Championship Shows where there has been anything from 7,000 to over 10,000 dogs present. It is an accolade that has come my way four times with four different dogs and these were moments that I will never forget. It must be the aim of all dedicated breeders and exhibitors and such success is indeed worth all the efforts of the past.

The exhibitors come from all walks of life. There can be few other sports that can claim such a cross-section of people. Exhibitors travel many thousands of miles during the year at no small cost and it lies in their hands to make a dog show a success or otherwise. Dog shows have to be a financial success, and it is the number of entries that makes the difference between profit and loss; nevertheless it is entirely the exhibitors' right to decide whether to come or stay away. For instance if a judge is known to have rather a heavy hand in handling dogs the exhibitors soon get to know this and it is very unlikely that they will trust their new puppies to that particular judge. Judges are very often known for putting up a certain type of dog in a particular breed, and if the exhibitors think that the judge's preference does not fit their particular type they will very obviously stay away. There are, of course, many other reasons why an exhibitor may not show under a certain judge, human nature being what it is; this sort of problem can be left to the reader's imagination.

As an exhibitor you will be sent an entrance pass, certainly for the larger shows, and on this entrance pass will be the bench number for your exhibit or exhibits. Catalogues are usually available at the entrance to the shows and these should give you any further information that you may require and that has not already been included in the schedule. The catalogue gives a detailed list of all entries and normally one of the first things that any exhibitor does is to purchase a catalogue so that the opposition can be weighed up. The discovery of who has entered and who has not can be both elating and depressing but the final say, of course, is for the judge. There is a chance for everyone, and few of us are not prepared to take it.

At most shows today after having exhibited your dog you are at liberty to leave the show. This is a new rule that is very much appreciated, as time for most of us is at a premium. Almost before we have left the show we are thinking of our next chance to try our luck. Showing is like a game of cards where fresh hope arrives with each new deal; how exciting it can all be.

CRUFT'S DOG SHOW

I have singled out this show because it is the Kennel Club's own show, and there are special qualifications enforced.

The founder of Cruft's was one Charles Cruft. He was born in 1852, the son of a jeweller, who like many other fathers hoped his son would follow in his footsteps. Charles was educated at Birkbeck College, and when he left in 1876 he joined James Spratt in his newly formed business of selling dog cakes. Spratt had recently returned from a trip to America where he had discovered this new dog food on the market. This had happened quite fortuitously as the result of a consignment of ship's biscuits being sold most successfully to dog owners.

Charles Cruft served his apprenticeship as an office boy but he soon progressed to be a salesman; his job was to visit the large estates where there were big kennels, and this particularly applied to the sporting breeds. He was successful, and in time he was sent to the Continent to call on kennels there. In 1878 he was invited by the French to undertake the organization of a canine section of the Paris Show. This was very successful and it brought further invitations to organize dog shows. In 1886 he managed the Allied Terrier Club Show held at the Royal Aquarium, Westminster, where there was an entry of 600 dogs.

Charles Cruft remained with Spratts for 30 years and became their General Manager. He had a special arrangement with his company that he could organize dog shows in his own right. In 1891 he booked the Royal Agricultural Hall, Islington, and this was the beginning of the Cruft's Shows. As there were no quarantine regulations in these days Cruft took the opportunity to bring over some of the rare breeds from the Continent and this naturally appealed to the visitors. It was said that he increased his bank balance very considerably and in these days the Kennel Club permitted individuals to run shows for their own personal gain.

Charles Cruft died in 1938. He had great talent and ability and when he died he was probably known to more people in the dog world than any other at that time. I wonder what he would have thought of the Cruft's Dog Show today?

Mr Cruft's widow organized one show in February 1939 but after that she felt it was too much for her and in 1942 she finalized an agreement with the Kennel Club to take over the future organization of Cruft's Dog Show. Six years later the first Cruft's Dog Show held under the management of the Kennel Club was held at Olympia.

Cruft's has a very special magic and draws crowds of spectators from all over the world. It is not the biggest dog show in Britain as several General Championship Shows can beat it, if that is the word, for actual numbers of dogs and entries. Cruft's in 1982 had a total entry of 9,844 dogs making 12,082 entries and from this grand collection of dogs there emerged as a shining star the little Toy Poodle Ch. Grayco Hazelnut owned by Mrs Leslie Howard. She was a very popular winner—many thought she had been very unlucky in 1981—and the vast crowd cheered her on to her great success.

Cruft's 1964 drew the largest entry of any Cruft's when no fewer than 8,277 dogs made an entry of 16,022. Space was at a premium and in 1965 the organizers decided to impose the first qualification for entry at Cruft's. This has been modified over the years and the qualifications for Cruft's 1983 are as follows:

(i) Entry in Breed Classes at Cruft's Show 1983 where Challenge Certificates are offered.

A dog is eligible for entry in breed classes where Challenge Certificates are offered if it has qualified in any of the following ways under the Rules and Regulations of the Kennel Club.

(a) If it is a Champion, Show Champion, Field Trial Champion, Working Trial Champion or Obedience Champion.

(b) If it has been awarded a Challenge Certificate at a show held between January 1, 1982 and December 13, 1982.

(c) If it has been awarded a Reserve Challenge Certificate at a Show held between January 1, 1982 and December 13, 1982.

(d) If it has won any of the following prizes in a breed class (as defined in Kennel Club Regulations for the Definitions of Classes at Championship Shows) at a Championship Show where Challenge Certificates were offered for the breed, between January 1, 1982 and December 13, 1982:
First in Minor Puppy Class, First in Puppy Class.
First in Junior Class, First in Post Graduate Class.
First in Limit Class, First in Open Class.
(subject to notes below).

(e) If it has won a first prize in the following classes at Cruft's Show, 1982. Special Puppy Class, Special Junior Class, Post Graduate Class, Limit Class, Open Class.

(f) If it has been awarded a 5-point or higher Green Star at a show held between January 1, 1982 and December 13, 1982 under Irish Kennel Club Rules and Regulations.

(g) If a Beagle, if it has won a first prize at a Hound Show between January 1, 1982 and December 13, 1982 held under the Rules of the Masters of Harriers and Beagles Association.

(ii) Entry in classes at Cruft's Show 1983 for Any Other Variety Not Separately Classified.

A dog is eligible for entry in classes for Any Other Variety Not Separately Classified if it has qualified in any of the following ways under the Rules and Regulations of the Kennel Club:

(a) If it has been declared Best of Sex or Reserve Best of Sex of a breed or gained any of the following prizes in Breed or Variety classes (as defined in the Kennel Club Regulations for the Definitions of Classes at Championship Shows) at a Championship Show held between January 1, 1982 and December 13, 1982.

First in Minor Puppy Class, First in Puppy Class,

First in Junior Class, First in Post Graduate Class,

First in Limit, First in Open.

(subject to notes below)

(b) If it has won a first prize in a class for Any Other Variety Not Separately Classified at Cruft's Show 1982.

(c) If it has been awarded a 5-point or higher Green Star at a Show held between January 1, 1982 and December 13, 1982 under Irish Kennel Club Rules and Regulations.

(iii) A dog is eligible for entry in Field Trial Classes if it has at any time won a prize, an Award of Honour, a Diploma of Merit or a Certificate of Merit in actual competition at a Field Trial held under Kennel Club or Irish Kennel Club Field Trial Rules and Regulations.

(iv) Obedience Championship at Cruft's Show 1983.

A dog is eligible for entry if it has won a Kennel Club Obedience Certificate at a Show held between January 1, 1982 and December 13, 1982.

Notes

1. A breed class is a class confined to one breed.

2. Qualifying awards as above in Minor Puppy, Puppy, Junior, Post Graduate, Limit and Open Classes qualify a dog for entry at Cruft's Show 1983 only if the class in which the award was gained was not made 'Special' in any way, i.e. by age, colour, height, weight, to members of a Society, to breeders, etc. An exception is made only in the case of prize winners in Special Puppy and Special Junior at Cruft's Show 1982. Wins in Brace, Team and Sweepstake Classes do not qualify nor do wins in any classes other than those stated above.

3. In any class scheduled at Cruft's Show 1983 for which an age limit appears in the definition, the age will be calculated to December 31, 1982, and not to the date of the show.

4. No entries will be accepted as 'Not for competition'.

5. Wins in breed classes at 1982 Championship Shows where Challenge Certificates are not offered will not qualify for entry in breed classes where Challenge Certificates are on offer at Cruft's Show 1983.

6. Dogs which gained Challenge Certificates prior to 1982 but have not qualified as above during the year will not be eligible for entry.

7. Eligibility of Champions is restricted to those whose title was gained

under Kennel Club Rules and Regulations.

8. Show awards which count towards the title of Champion under the Rules of any governing body other than the Kennel Club will not count as qualification for Cruft's 1983 except the award of a 5-point or higher Green Star at a Show held between January 1, 1982 and December 13, 1982 under Irish Kennel Club Rules and Regulations.

Exhibitors and breeders aim to qualify their stock for Cruft's although they may not eventually enter them at the show, as by the time the show comes along a bitch could be having or have had puppies. Coated breeds can be out of coat and bitches can be in season and although this is not a disqualification many breeders do not like to risk showing their bitch at this time. Other domestic reasons can prevent dogs qualified from coming to Cruft's and although it is perhaps not the most popular show with exhibitors, due mainly to the crowds of people that swarm around the benches all day giving the dogs little rest, there is no question that it is amongst the great sporting events of the calendar. Being in London, and I am not suggesting that it should ever be in any other spot away from the capital, it is a difficult show for exhibitors to park their cars near and there is no green grass to exercise the dogs on; but still they come and still they travel many miles during the year just to qualify their dogs for the one and only Cruft's.

Cruft's has had a woman at the helm since 1978: she is Mrs Jacqueline Hollis, the Show Manager. I wonder what Charles Cruft would have thought of that?

QUALIFICATIONS FOR A DOG SHOW JUDGE

As already explained, there are various different types of show, from the Exemption Shows to the Limited and Sanction Shows, then on to the Open Shows and so to the Championship Shows. The Kennel Club approves all judges for Championship Shows as at these shows it is the Kennel Club's own Challenge Certificates that are on offer. For all other shows anyone can judge, and I mean anyone, provided they get an invitation from the Secretary of the Show organizing the event under Kennel Club Rules and Regulations.

With some 3,000 shows per year it would be an impossible task for the Kennel Club to approve every judge for every show. It is an enormous task to approve all Championship Show judges—453 shows in 1982—without even attempting to govern those judging at Open and

Limited Shows. The Kennel Club have a special Committee called the Judges' Sub-committee and this Committee approve or reject the names put before it. These decisions go forward to the Executive Committee of the Kennel Club for their final confirmation. All names of new judges must be submitted by the show society to the Kennel Club at least nine months before the show for which they are asking approval. For judges that have previously awarded Challenge Certificates in a particular breed the time is six months. Show Organizing Secretaries must work at least one year ahead to ensure compliance with these Kennel Club Regulations.

The shows at which judges gain experience to qualify them to give Challenge Certificates are Limited and Open Shows. Some Open Shows in Britain extend to 200 classes and are much bigger than many Championship Shows in other countries. Judges gain vast experience in judging breeds and variety classes at Open Shows and can judge anything between 200 and 300 dogs and sometimes more, on one day. This makes for excellent training.

Unlike those of some other countries, judges in Britain are not expected to qualify by written examination; I am sure this is reasonable. Some of our very best judges, alas no longer with us, would never have been able to pass even the simplest written test but most of us would have had complete confidence in them and happily trusted them to advise on the purchase of any dog. If we had been deprived of these 'greats' because of their inability to pass a written examination we would have been deprived of the great knowledge they passed on to their younger colleagues; the dog world would have been the poorer.

Championship Show judges in the United Kingdom are never given approval to judge a block of breeds within a Group just because they have already been approved to judge say seventy-five per cent of the breeds. This is not enough. The ability to judge every breed must be individually approved on the judge's experience of that breed, or rejected for the lack of it. It is a long hard road to the top, involving years of intensive study, years of travelling up and down the country most weekends to get the necessary practical experience, and years of just being with dogs to learn all about them.

When a judge is invited to judge a breed at a Championship Show for the first time with Kennel Club Challenge Certificates, the Society inviting the judge must issue a Kennel Club questionnaire to the judge for completion. This should then be approved by the Society concerned and forwarded to the Kennel Club for their approval. In most breeds the Kennel Club expect the applicant to have judged for about five years at Open Shows. The experience of the applicant is also looked at in respect of what stock has been bred and how successful that stock has been in the show ring. If the applicant is already approved to award Challenge Certificates in other breeds this is also taken into consideration. Breed Clubs of the particular breed applied for are asked by the Kennel Club for their opinion and all the information available about the applicant comes before the Kennel Club Judges Sub-committee.

The approval or non-approval of judges to judge at Championship Shows will always be a controversial subject, particularly, of course, with those not approved for one reason or another.

Systems vary slightly throughout the world; but although overseas adjudicators are welcome in the UK, and some very fine judges come from abroad, they do not automatically get approval in Britain even if they award Challenge Certificates to a particular breed in their own country.

In America the system is very similar to the British, and British judges are permitted to award American Kennel Club Certificates in those breeds that they are approved to judge in Britain; and in most cases the reverse is true.

There is certainly a 'jet set' of judges and with air travel as it is today there is a continual exchange of judges all round the world. This International Panel of Judges can do nothing but good for dog shows and show dogs and although dogs themselves are not permitted to travel so freely, at least travelling judges can compare the quality of dogs in other countries with the quality at home, and I am sure that many of us do just this.

Dogs coming into Britain from abroad need to undergo a period of six months' quarantine in Ministry-approved quarantine kennels. Apart from the time factor, this is quite a costly business when one takes into account first the price of the dog, secondly the freight to get it into the quarantine kennels and thirdly the cost of boarding for the six months. This precludes the great majority of dogs from abroad from competing in our shows but not all, as breeders wishing to improve their stock do think that all the cost in money and time is well worth while in bringing in a dog from overseas. I personally have done it twice and at the time of writing have a third dog in quarantine.

Much as I would like to see International Shows with dogs from all countries competing I know that this would be inadvisable as the chance of spreading rabies to countries that are free of this scourge at the moment would never justify the tremendous risk.

We must be content with the comparisons drawn by our judges and written about in the dog press, and the marvellous colour pictures that appear in the annuals published throughout the world.

12

Ailments, accidents & suggested treatments

With reasonable care and attention dogs should be healthy animals. The only sad fact is that their life span is only a fraction of our own expectation; but during that short time they should enjoy good health and be happy members of our community.

Once you have acquired a puppy, be it a show specimen or just a lovable member of your household, it is wise for you to know where to find a good Veterinary Surgeon if the need arises. If you need advice on this ask a local dog breeder as no matter what breed they may specialize in they should be able to recommend a suitable veterinarian who specializes in small animals. This is particularly important if you intend to breed from your animal; it is no good waiting for trouble, particularly in the middle of the night, before making contact with a Veterinary Surgeon. Having found and introduced yourself to a Veterinary Surgeon do not bother him/her unduly; use your common sense, as you would with your Doctor. If you have a bitch in whelp then warn him of the due date. Then he will not be too surprised if he has to make a visit at some ungodly hour. It is so often at these hours that things begin to happen.

A dog's temperature is usually a very good guide to his overall health. Individual animals, like humans, can vary slightly but the temperature should be in the region of 38.5°C or 101.5°F. If your dog appears off-colour, for example not eating his food with his usual relish, generally listless and lethargic, in any way irritable, or showing signs of diarrhoea or a discharge from the eyes or nose, take his temperature immediately and if it is either up or down by a degree or two it is usually wise to seek your Veterinary Surgeon's advice.

A dog's temperature should be taken with a blunt-ended clinical thermometer the end of which should first of all be smeared with Vaseline. Special veterinary thermometers are available that do indicate the various correct temperatures for different animals such as

114

dogs, horses, cats etc. and these are most helpful. Before inserting the thermometer shake it to make sure that it registers a low reading otherwise you could get a false result which might alarm you and cause unnecessary trouble. The thermometer should be held in place for at least the time stated on it and should have half its length in the rectum. A very gentle pressure on the dog's anus by the thermometer will help relax the dog's muscles and allow it to slip in quite comfortably. Never force the thermometer but use gentle pressure at all times. When you have left it in long enough withdraw it and hold it horizontally twisting it round until the reading becomes quite clear. After use the thermometer should be cleaned by wiping it with a piece of cotton wool that has been soaked in surgical spirit and then put back into its own container ready for use again.

A low temperature reading can be even more serious than a high one and it is well to remember this fact. In nursing sick animals it is imperative that they should be kept spotlessly clean, warm and quiet, and given their prescribed treatment with understanding and great patience; this will encourage them at all times to help themselves to feel better.

To get your dog to take a dose of medicine get him to stand or sit in front of you and if possible have someone to help you try and keep him steady. With the fingers of your left hand pull down the right-hand corner of his bottom lip and gently pour the medicine into his mouth. Close his mouth and hold it shut, at the same time slightly tipping it upwards. Gently stroke his throat until he swallows the medicine and of course thereafter tell him how good he has been. Never ever open his mouth and attempt to throw the liquid down it. He will be quicker than you and more than likely you will get a share of the medicine thrown back at you. This rather crude method of making him take his medicine could indeed make him choke and be sick apart altogether from the sudden shock of an unpleasant-tasting substance being thrown into his mouth.

The same method should be employed when your dog has to have a pill. Gently open his mouth, quickly put the pill on the back of his tongue and shut his mouth immediately. Keep his head held high, very gently stroke his throat and when he swallows the pill should go down. Some dogs get rather adept at somehow very quickly placing the pill in the side of their mouth; when they swallow the pill stays put and does not go down. If this method proves difficult try putting the pill in a bit of meat or some other delicacy that your dog loves and hope that when he swallows the favoured morsel the pill will go down with it. Always remember to give due praise to the dog when he has taken his medicine or pill and so let him know that he has pleased you—this alone will give him confidence.

AN A–Z OF PROBLEMS

Accidents

Accidents will happen even in the best-regulated households and one should at least know what to do if the occasion arises. If your dog has an accident, perhaps a collision with a car, keep him absolutely quiet, moving him as little as possible and seek veterinary treatment straightaway. Where there may be an internal or external haemorrhage it is most unwise to give a stimulant such as brandy. This could perhaps be better applied to the owner of the dog who will obviously be distressed at the sight of his beloved companion in pain and discomfort.

If your dog has cut his foot or leg badly bandage the wound as tightly as possible to try to arrest the bleeding and apply a tourniquet somewhere between the wound and the heart. To tighten the tourniquet push a pencil or bit of wood through the bandage and twist it. Always remember that at this stage when the dog is under great strain and suffering pain he might try to bite even his best friend, and quite without malice. To avoid this tape his mouth with a bandage or even an old silk stocking before attempting to treat him. To tape the dog it is necessary to put the tape round his mouth a couple of times and then bring it under his throat, cross it over, and bring it up on to his neck where you tie it very firmly. This will not hurt the dog, and it will safeguard you and allow you more freely to treat the dog.

For abrasions, slight cuts and generally minor accidents, clean the wound and dry it with cotton wool; then smear it with calamine or zinc ointment, or better still penicillin ointment if obtainable, although normally this is only available on prescription.

Never attempt to bandage a wound on a dog unless it is absolutely essential because he will only try to get the bandage off and so often cause more damage than has already been done. If bandages have to be used some restrictive measure will have to be taken and the use of a plastic bucket can solve this problem. Take the bottom out of the plastic bucket and make holes round the bottom edge of the bucket; by threading strong string through these holes and on to the dog's leather collar the bucket should be quite securely fastened to the collar. Pass

116

the bucket over the dog's head and fasten his collar on in the usual way. With his head in the bucket the dog cannot get to its wound and although this may look terribly uncomfortable, and I am sure it is, this does allow the wound to heal as quickly as possible and without any further interference from the dog. This, in my opinion is certainly a much better method than muzzling the dog as with a muzzle he will still try to rub the wound and finish up with a nasty mess which will take even longer to heal.

Blood coming from an artery is bright red in colour and will spurt in unison with the heartbeat. Blood coming from a vein is dark red and continuous in flow.

Anal glands

With a correct diet and where the motions are solid it is unlikely that these glands will give any trouble. I have found that generally the Toy Group of dogs are more susceptible to anal gland problems than their bigger brothers and sister. The anal glands are situated on either side of the anal opening and if they become infected they can be a nuisance to the dog and cause discomfort and irritation. The symptoms are easily recognizable as the dog will keep turning round to lick his bottom and drag it along the ground as though he was trying to relieve himself of an irritation. In severe cases the dog will tuck his tail down covering his anus and look thoroughly miserable. A slight discharge and rather an unpleasant smell indicate badly infected and impacted glands.

If you feel unable to cope with this yourself take your dog along to your Veterinary Surgeon so that he can squeeze the glands and rid them of their unsavoury contents. If you wish to treat the condition yourself take a fairly large pad of cotton wool in your right hand and hold the dog by his tail or back-end with your left hand. Put the cotton wool over the offending glands and gently press inwards and then upwards with your thumb and forefinger. This action should get rid of the matter from the glands but if the dog still seems to suffer discomfort take him along to the Veterinarian. This condition must not be allowed to persist as it can result in anal abscesses which are unpleasant, difficult to clear and in the meantime cause your dog further suffering. As far as your dog's health is concerned a good rule to be guided by is never to put off until tomorrow what you can attend to today.

Arthritis

This is a disease involving a joint or the inflammation of a joint.

117

Normally it is confined to our older dogs but it can make the dog quite unhappy and lame just as it does humans. Rest and warmth are essential and fortunately nowadays pills can be prescribed to help the pain. We have many older dogs in our kennel and they all have their 'sweets' to help them overcome the problems that arise with any geriatric.

Bites
If your dog is bitten by another dog, or another animal, cleanse the wound very thoroughly with some warm water to which an antiseptic has been added. It is essential that the wound should be kept open until all discharge stops. Apply penicillin ointment or, if this is not available, tincture of iodine. When there is no further discharge a healing ointment can be used. If the wound is deep and nasty take your dog to your Veterinary Surgeon as it may require a stitch or two and it may also be wise to have your animal given an injection to prevent or halt any infection.

   If your dog is bitten by a snake a bandage should be applied as soon as possible and as tightly as possible above the affected part, i.e. between the bite and the heart. This should at least help prevent the poison from spreading into the bloodstream. Try to squeeze out the poison, but waste as little time as possible in getting the animal to your Veterinary Surgeon.

Burns and scalds
Any dog living in a house must run the risk of being burned or scalded as, if allowed, they can get beneath one's feet in the kitchen where such accidents are likely to occur. If the burn is at all serious do not delay in either taking your dog to the Veterinary Hospital or calling for professional help. In the meantime the dog should be kept warm and quiet and not left alone. He should be wrapped up in a blanket as there is always the risk of shock to be taken into account. To treat a minor burn, gently clean the burn, removing any foreign matter such as straw or dirt, and then as quickly as possible exclude all air from it by applying olive oil or any oily substance. Cover this with dry gauze, cotton wool and a loose bandage. Most households now carry in their first aid kit lotions for use in the case of first degree burns to humans and these can equally be applied to dogs when the burn is of a minor nature. To stop your dog licking his injury it may well be necessary to apply a hood (see page 116).

The excitement of winning

ABOVE
All miniature Dachshunds must be weighed
to ensure that they come within the weight
standard of 5kg/11lb. In Britain this is the
judge's responsibility

The final of the Hound Group at the
Scottish Kennel Club Centenary Show in
1981

LEFT
Dogs travel much more happily and safely
in their crates or boxes

Giving an injection

A plastic bucket can help stop a dog biting its wounds, and so enable them to heal more quickly

The correct way to administer pills: *left*, hold mouth firmly and drop the pill well into the back of the throat; *right*, shut the mouth quickly, and rub the throat till the dog swallows

ABOVE
The correct way to take a dog's
temperature; if necessary the end of the
thermometer should be steadied with the
hand

Show dogs can also be very good working
dogs, as the Boxer demonstrates

Best of Breed Elkhound — Ravenna, Ohio, USA

Best of Breed St Bernard, Lompoc Valley
Kennel Club, California, 26 July 1980

Canker

This is more common in long-eared breeds and is caused by tiny parasites getting into the canal of the ear and multiplying rapidly. They cause tremendous discomfort to the dog and when your dog persists in scratching the ear, before you know what has happened he has torn the ear on the outside. He will go on doing this until treatment is prescribed. Don't think because he is scratching the outside of his ear that he has some irritation there. The trouble in nearly every case is inside the ear, often deep down, and not on the outside surface.

The ear is a very delicate organ and it is best not to waste any time by trying some old pet cure. Take your dog to your Veterinary Surgeon and he will prescribe proper treatment and also show you the correct manner to apply it. Never poke down into an ear with anything, as this is likely to damage the ear. Even by poking your finger down you can do more damage than good.

When you notice that your dog is scratching around his ear, if you care to smell inside his ear you will find that it is horrible and evil-smelling. In such cases you can be sure that your dog has either wet or dry canker; both need immediate remedial treatment. If either condition is allowed to persist it will become quite chronic and only an operation, an aural resection, will make amends. Although this puts the dog to great discomfort for a limited period it is nearly always a success. The best way to avoid this is to ensure that during regular grooming periods you check on your dog's ears to see that they are healthy and clean and in the end save yourself unnecessary expense, and your dog unnecessary pain and discomfort.

Colic

This is a very severe pain in the abdomen and is usually due to indigestion, flatulence or constipation. It is generally thought to be caused by incorrect feeding and is a complaint suffered more often by the larger dogs. The pain does not usually linger for long but quite long enough to make the dog very unhappy and restless. Symptoms quite often appear after a heavy meal when the dog seems to swell up and look bloated. Veterinary attention must be sought immediately in such cases and only very prompt action can save the life of your dog. In severe cases where the dog appears bloated try to relieve the tension until treatment is at hand by giving your dog a piece of washing soda about the size of a walnut. This will make him vomit and release some

119

of the gas in his stomach.

The cause of this ailment is still unknown but there are three very simple precautions that you can take to help avoid this condition. Never give your dog heavy meals late at night, never feed him with unsoaked biscuit meal and never feed him with food that is served too wet. Try not to forget these three golden rules.

Constipation

Once again this problem is usually caused by an unbalanced diet. The dog finds difficulty in passing his stools which are very hard and dry. With this condition a change of diet should be tried and also ask yourself if your dog is getting enough proper exercise. If these measures do not rectify the problem then a gentle laxative should be given. This can be liquid paraffin or milk of magnesia in small doses over a period of time.

Coprophagy

Dogs sometimes suffer from this complaint—eating their own faeces. The suggested cures for this rather nasty habit are many and varied. Some say that the cause of the trouble is a vitamin deficiency, others say that it is an iron deficiency. I think the best cure is to make sure that faeces are not left lying around to give the dog the opportunity to eat them. Most dogs will devour the faeces of cows and horses, if given the chance, and do so with relish. Prevention in this case, I feel, is better than any cure that may be suggested.

Corns

These are sometimes found on the heavier breeds with no long coats to protect their skins. Usually corns appear on the elbows or the hocks but can be prevented by ensuring that the dog has a comfortable bed and that he does not lie around on a hard floor or concrete. If you think that your dog may be developing a corn it is a good idea to rub the spot with surgical spirit. This will help harden the skin and so prevent the unsightly corn growing. There are plenty of different kinds of good comfortable beds on the market nowadays and there is really little excuse for this condition particularly with dogs that live in the house.

Dandruff

This is a scurfy condition of the skin and coat and very often due to neglect of the coat and insufficient proper grooming. If regular

120

grooming takes place this will increase the circulation to the skin, thus stimulating the nerve supply and generally improving its condition. This condition can also be ascribed to a badly balanced diet and lack of exercise. The feeding of a dog is very much reflected in his coat and if his coat looks dull and dreary, scurfy and full of dandruff, then you can be sure that you have your dog on a wrong diet and the sooner you change it the better. To help this condition a good coat oil can be used and it must be well rubbed in. This is a condition very rarely found in show dogs. After all the show ring is a place for beauty. No beauty queen would ever win if she was not groomed and dressed to perfection. So it is with show dogs.

Diarrhoea

In puppies this can be the result of worms but it can also be caused by a change of diet particularly when a puppy leaves the kennel he was born in to go to his new home. If worms are suspected it is necessary to ascertain whether they are of the round or tape variety as they require different remedies. There are many perfectly safe preparations on the market that can be used to eradicate these pests. All puppies should have been wormed at least twice before leaving their place of birth but even so it may well be that some of these pests stay with them; unless they are got rid of they will quickly multiply again. They must be eradicated to ensure the steady growth of your puppy.

If worms are not the cause of the diarrhoea and it persists, a Veterinary Surgeon must be consulted. Diarrhoea can be the beginning of another more serious ailment, such as distemper, hard-pad or parvo-virus, and the sooner it is attended to the better.

Distemper

Canine distemper is due to a virus that invades the nervous system; it is a highly contagious disease. Through modern research dogs can now be inoculated with preventive serums and every dog lover is failing in his or her duty if such action is not taken as soon as a puppy is old enough, usually between 10 and 12 weeks. The symptoms are usually a very high temperature and a discharge from the nose, often followed by a cough. The dog will appear completely listless and very unhappy. Fits often follow and even paralysis; if the disease gets to this stage it is seldom curable. Never ever take such an affected dog to the Canine Hospital. This will only spread the infection and such an infection can travel fast enough anyway without your helping it. Your Veterinary

Surgeon should be asked to call at your home. If the dog has any hope of recovering he will require very careful and dedicated nursing at all hours of the day and night. Much better to ensure that the dog has full immunity as soon as possible.

Ears

We have already described Canker: this term is often used by the layman as a description for anything that affects the ear. Sore ears that have been badly scratched are usually the result of carelessness on the owner's part as ulceration, which is seen as sores that are discharging pus, cannot just happen overnight. As already said, check ears at least once a week for any possible problems and stop them before they catch hold.

Entropion

This is very much more common in some breeds, such as Chows, than in others. If a puppy has a weepy eye check more carefully and you will very often find that the lids are curled inwards in such a way that the lashes are irritating the eyeball itself. This condition appears to be hereditary and only an operation can put the matter right.

External parasites

If a dog is allowed free-range exercise in fields or woods he is bound to pick up fleas, lice or ticks. If you find that your dog has collected some of these pests there are many brands of louse powder on the market that will soon eradicate them. Do remember that not only the dog must be treated but his bedding and other habitual places of rest. Fleas and lice can be the start of skin troubles and general disability. The sooner you get rid of them the better. They can be very persistent but if you follow the instructions given on the packet you should be successful

Eyes

The eye is a very delicate organ and when you are giving any treatment to it care must be taken at all times to handle gently and not to exert any undue pressure on it. A slight discharge may be caused by the dog's lying in a draught or he may have caught a slight cold in his eye. It should be very carefully wiped away with cotton wool or a tissue and the eye bathed with cotton wool dipped in lukewarm boracic solution. If this condition persists then take your dog along for veterinary treatment as it could be a symptom of a more serious disease and the sooner it is attended to by a skilled person the better.

If a foreign body gets into the eye (grass seeds have a bad habit of doing just this) bathe the eye very gently with the above solution and try to remove the offending particle. The eye could appear rather red and swollen. If your dog is unfortunate enough to get an acid of some sort in his eyes immediately make a purse of the eyelids and pour in some castor oil or glycerine.

On no account should a dog ever be allowed to hang his head out of the car window. This is simply asking for trouble and eye colds with serious consequences can be the result.

Feet

Split pads and eczema will cause a dog to nibble at his feet and if this is allowed to continue will result in lameness. Gentian violet, now supplied in spray form, should be applied. These sores can take some time to heal and do cause the dog discomfort and pain. Inflamed toes can be caused by the nail being caught and partially torn out and this also applies to dew claws. I always feel that these are best removed when the puppy is about three or four days old (see page 36). Soak the paw in a warm antiseptic solution as often as possible and this will ease the pain as the paw becomes very tender. Try to keep the paw as clean as possible.

Cysts between the toes can be a perfect nuisance as they too cause lameness. Treatment in this case should be sought from your Veterinary Surgeon as they may require surgery.

If your dog happens to pick up some tar on his feet during the hot weather this can cause him great discomfort. The hair should be cut away from between the toes and a substantial amount of fat, lard or margarine rubbed well into his toes to soften the tar. Thereafter the feet can be thoroughly washed.

Fits

These can be caused by very many things, some associated with virus diseases. Veterinary help must be sought immediately.

Haematoma

This blood-serum blister is usually a side effect caused by the dog scratching himself for some reason or it can be caused by a bang or a blow. Unlike an abscess, such a swelling is soft at first and only later on does a rather hard edge form. Haematomatas are most common on the ear as many games players have found. They usually clear by themselves but if not surgical treatment might be necessary.

Hard pad disease

This is very similar to distemper and as already said all dogs should have their inoculations against this disease when they are puppies. Canine encephalitis is caused by a virus and usually attacks the central nervous system. If the animal survives he is usually left with a thickening and hardening of the skin on the pads and sometimes on the nose—hence the name 'hard pad'.

Hiccough

Some dogs are susceptible to this complaint and although it is not a serious one it distresses the dog while it lasts. It is more common in puppies than in adults and is usually the result of indigestion or an irritation that is caused by worms. Bicarbonate of soda in milk usually brings some relief.

Hip displasia

This is a very controversial subject today and whilst some breeds seem to be completely free from it others are not. This deformity is not easy to diagnose. I have seen many dogs with a bad gait that some would say have hip displasia but when X-rayed they are found to be free. On the other hand I have known dogs that have moved extremely accurately but whose X-rays show them to have this malformation of the hip joint. The only safe way to diagnose the complaint is by X-ray. Dogs with hip displasia can live to a great age and they can be just as active as dogs who have correct hips and just as happy. Hip displasia is no serious impediment for a family pet that is not to be bred from. Many authorities believe that hip displasia is not always hereditary but often due to bad environment, rearing and exercise.

Kennel cough

This has in recent years become more widespread and there is no question that it is contagious. Fortunately its effects on most dogs are not serious but, of course, there is the odd case when a dog reacts to it very badly. It can be a problem in a large kennel as it quickly passes from one dog to another and goes round in a circle. If young puppies catch the infection it can take a great toll on their general health when they are growing and can do without this encumbrance. Adult dogs do not generally worry much about it and provided they are in good condition usually manage to throw it off quite quickly. Treatment, if necessary, can consist of a mild expectorant with codeine and perhaps an anti-histamine. Dogs suffering from kennel cough should be isolated and certainly never taken to shows or other places where they can meet other dogs and pass it on. Antibiotics can be given by a Veterinary Surgeon to prevent any secondary infections as it is so often these secondary infections that prove troublesome. As yet there is no fully effective inoculation against kennel cough.

Leptospirosis

There are two different forms of this unpleasant disease. Leptospiral jaundice is caused by food fouled by rats carrying the virus. The symptoms are fever, diarrhoea and listlessness with bleeding gums and sometimes a bleeding nose. The actual jaundice, as in humans, does not become apparent until a later date. An inoculation is available to prevent this disease and this can be given at the same time as the distemper and hard pad injections. This is a very serious complaint and no time must be wasted in calling for the help of your Veterinary Surgeon. Leptospiral nephritis, like the jaundice, is a very serious disease that attacks the tissue of the kidneys. Symptoms are again a high temperature, lethargy and complete loss of appetite. An affected dog tends to roach his back and look as though he is in some considerable pain particularly from his kidneys. He will have an excessive thirst and bad breath and seem to have some difficulty in passing urine. Once again you need your Veterinary Surgeon's help but prevention is better than cure and the puppy should have been injected against this scourge.

Metritis

This is caused by the retention of membranes and afterbirth when a bitch has finished whelping. The trouble can soon be rectified by your Veterinary Surgeon who will give an injection of pituitrin to get rid of this waste, followed by a course of some other drug to clear up any internal infection.

Nettlerash (*Urticaria*)

This is not serious but if you have not seen it before it can be quite alarming. The dog's head swells, lumps appear all over his body and naturally he looks rather pathetic. It does not usually affect the dog's

125

well being or his appetite and is caused by some allergy just as in humans. Urticaria will go down of its own accord within a short space of time and requires no treatment.

Poisoning
Great speed must be employed in expelling any poison swallowed by a dog. Simple emetics are the best, e.g. washing soda, or salt and water.

Rheumatism
Just like humans, dogs can be subject to this complaint and can suffer severe pain if it is a bad attack. Aspirins administered to the dog three or four times a day usually put an end to his discomfort.

Rickets
This is due to bad rearing and the outcome of malnutrition. Prevention is much better than any cure. The term 'rickets' implies that the bones of a puppy have not formed correctly. This is entirely due to the bad rearing of the puppy or of his dam. The indications are crooked, knobbly joints, bowed legs and generally a malformed appearance. In advanced cases the bones become soft and are very easily broken.

Shock
As in humans this is something that should never be treated lightly. It can arise after a severe injury or an accident and the dog should be kept as warm as possible. A dog should not be persuaded to swallow any liquid unless it is fully conscious. If he will take a spot of brandy or whisky by himself this can be beneficial. A dog in shock will appear completely prostrated and his breathing will be very shallow. His eyes will have a glassy look with the pupils generally dilated.

Electric wires should be kept out of reach of dogs and puppies, but if this safeguard has not been taken always remember to disconnect the electricity before touching the animal. If the dog's heart is still beating, although he might appear to have stopped breathing, start artificial respiration at once. This is done by placing the dog on his right side with head and neck extended and tongue drawn forward. The hand is then placed over the ribs immediately behind the shoulder blade. A sudden steady downward movement of the hand causes the chest to be compressed and the air in the lungs to be expelled. The pressure is released immediately allowing the chest to expand by its own elasticity and so fill with air. This procedure should be repeated at intervals of about five seconds.

Skin conditions

These are many and varied but to the layman most skin troubles seem to carry the tag of 'mange'. In fact, the only way to be sure of the diagnosis is for a Veterinary Surgeon to take a proper skin scraping.

Sarcoptic mange is caused by a very active little parasite and is very contagious. It can easily be transmitted by means of grooming tools, bedding, kennels etc. The parasite usually attacks the skin around the eyes, the outside of the ears, the skin covering the abdomen and the elbows. Small red spots, looking rather like flea bites, appear and the acrid matter they excrete sets up intense irritation causing the dog to scratch and bite himself. Sores and bare patches appear and the dog suffers a tremendous amount of discomfort. It is readily cured with modern drugs such as tetmosol and benzyl benzoate.

Follicular mange usually starts with a single bare patch of a dirty greyish colour like the coat of an elephant. Unlike sarcoptic mange little or no irritation is caused but there is no question that this is similarly a parasitic condition and under the microscope the parasite looks like a small maggot. Some think that this skin condition is not contagious but congenital, i.e. passed on from generation to generation. This type of mange is very much more difficult to cure than sarcoptic and you must seek the help of your Veterinary Surgeon.

Eczema is a non-contagious skin disease that many believe to be dietary in cause. I also believe that it can be a nervous condition. I well remember a Bulldog coming in to board in our own kennels. He arrived in perfect condition with no sign of any skin trouble. About one hour after his arrival it was noticed that he was rather restless and on inspection it was discovered that a small spot of wet eczema had started across his shoulders. By the afternoon he was practically covered in this condition and the only cause that we could put it down to was the change in his environment—he had not even been fed so that there was no question of a change in diet being responsible. The skin is irritable and the dog scratches and bites at himself continuously which, of course, makes the condition worse and it spreads very rapidly. The affected area becomes sticky with a discharge and hair must be cut away from this sticky part. The dog may have to wear a hood to stop him getting at the affected part. We have always found benzyl benzoate or an alternative ointment successful in clearing this condition.

Skin troubles are not easy to diagnose and one should never jump to a conclusion before a full report has been received from your Veterinary Surgeon. Some forms of dermatitis and other skin eruptions caused by a simple allergy can look like mange.

To avoid any of these skin troubles make sure that your dog is given a correct diet, proper exercise and regular grooming.

Slavering

A dog that suddenly starts to slaver should be examined to find the explanation. It could very well be that a small piece of bone has become stuck in his mouth, between his teeth or across his palate. So often he can manage to get rid of the offending object with his paw but if he is having some difficulty he would appreciate your help.

Stings

If your dog is stung (some dogs have a bad habit of trying to snap at bees or wasps), try to locate the exact spot of the sting and extract it as soon as possible. If it is a bee sting treat it with TCP or bicarbonate of soda. If it is a wasp sting treat the spot with vinegar or any mild acid. In both cases it is very wise to have your dog injected with an anti-histamine which will give quick relief.

Sunstroke or heatstroke

In a hot summer this condition can be quite common but here again the prevention is better than the cure. If you intend to leave your dog in his outside kennel and run you must make sure that you have provided him with adequate shade from the sun. Also make sure that at all times he has access to a plentiful supply of cold water.

If dogs are confined in a vehicle which is exposed to the sun sunstroke or heatstroke will very soon arise. The signs are excessive panting with profuse salivation followed by weakness of the limbs, a staggering gait and final collapse. Get the dog to a cool place at once and apply ice and cold water to his head, neck and shoulders. I once saved a well-known Champion dog at a dog show by taking him to a tank of cold water and plunging him into it leaving just his head above the surface. I held him there for a few minutes and then took him to rest in a cool spot under some trees. Soon he was able to take some cool water and to everyone's relief recovered quite quickly but it was a very near thing. Prompt action is necessary.

Tails

If your dog lives in a kennel and he is a breed with a long tail, he may persistently wag it, hitting the kennel wall or door; the tail can soon become very raw and start to bleed. If this persists in bad cases the top of the tail will have to be amputated. This problem arises mostly with the larger breeds such as Irish Wolfhounds, Greyhounds and Great Danes. If your dog has a sore at the end of his tail try to harden the skin with surgical spirit. There is now such a thing on the market as a tail guard which can be a great help if the dog will keep it on! Otherwise the tail should be dressed each day, padded with cotton wool and bandaged; the dressing should then be made more secure by the use of adhesive tape or sticky plaster.

Teeth

Dogs should not be troubled with bad teeth if they are given a correct diet. Sometimes in puppies the milk teeth are reluctant to make way for the permanent teeth. The fact that these baby teeth are still intact could make the second teeth come in out of alignment and so spoil the puppy's chance in the show ring. It is best to take the puppy to your Veterinary Surgeon so that the offending teeth can be removed to allow the permanent teeth to have their rightful place. If such an exercise has to take place I always ask my Veterinary Surgeon to remove the teeth under a general anaesthetic so that the puppy is not conscious of someone handling his mouth and making it painful and sore. Show dogs have their mouths examined by the judge and if a dog remembers some nasty experience in respect of his mouth he will be reluctant to allow the judge to examine it without fuss and so spoil his chances of winning.

Older dogs may have to have their teeth scaled and tooth-scalers are available if you wish to do this yourself. Take the scaler and place the end of the tool at the base of the tooth between the gum and the scale. Draw the tool down the tooth quite firmly and the scale should come away leaving a clean tooth.

Stained teeth caused by distemper or some other virus cannot be scaled. They are permanently marked and the stains will not come off.

Travel sickness

This is quite common in dogs but we have found with show dogs that after a few journeys they nearly all settle and get over this problem. For those that persist in being sick there are many good remedies on the market to help—it is just a question of finding out what suits your dog best. It is a good idea to get puppies used to travelling in the car—short trips to begin with and then longer journeys—and the majority of them simply adore being with you and think nothing of car journeys.

Tuberculosis

This is not a very common disease in dogs. The condition is revealed by a nasty chronic cough and he will lose condition and become rather thin. If his temperature is taken it will be found to be subnormal. In dogs it is a difficult disease to cure but with the help of modern drugs I am sure your veterinary surgeon will do his best.

Worms

It is most unusual for puppies not to have worms. These are round worms or *Toxocara canis*. These should be eradicated when the puppy is young otherwise their presence will stunt its proper growth. Adult dogs suffer more from tapeworm infestation. Whether their presence is suspected or not it is always advisable to treat them for this condition at regular intervals. If there are no worms the medicine will only act as an aperient always provided the correct dosage is administered—this is very important. There are many safe worming preparations now on the market but it is essential that the dose accurate for the size of the dog or the age of the puppy is given. Follow the instructions on the package very strictly and if you are in any doubt whatsoever contact your Veterinary Surgeon.

The usual symptoms of tapeworm infestation are either depleted or increased appetite, loss of coat condition or a nasty smelling breath.

Although roundworms and tapeworms are the most common worms there are others that can invade your dog. The most common of these are whipworms, hookworms and heartworms. These are more difficult to get rid of but it is equally important that they be eradicated and if you are at all uncertain that your dog is clear of worms the best thing to do is to send a specimen of your dog's faeces to your Veterinary Surgeon for analysis. The result of this will ensure that the correct treatment can be prescribed.

Glossary

Glossary

Abdomen The belly of the dog or that portion of the body that lies between the chest and the pelvis.

Achilles tendon The tendon that attaches the muscle in the second thigh to the bone below the hock.

Action The movement of the dog—the way it walks, trots or runs.

Affixes These are normally attached to a dog's registered name in order to identify him with a particular kennel. The kennel owner pays an annual fee for this or can pay in Britain, a lump sum to the Kennel Club for the lifetime of the owner. When the kennel name is before the dog's name this is known as a prefix and when after the dog's name a suffix.

Albino An animal which suffers from a deficiency of pigment in the skin and hair, which are always white, and in the eyes which are generally pink. More common in white dogs.

Almond eye Eyelids in the shape of an almond.

Angulation Angles formed by the joints with special reference to the forehand and the quarters.

Anus Outlet at the end of the rectum.

Apple-headed With a skull that is rounded or very domed.

Apron Long hair on the chest of the dog.

Back That part of the dog's body between withers and set-on of tail along vertebrae.

Bad doer A dog that no matter how well cared for will not put on any condition. Very often they are very fussy and poor eaters.

Balance Every part of the body in proportion.

Barrel ribs Barrel-shaped ribs, almost circular in contour.

Bat ears Erect ears, broad at base, rounded or semi-rounded at tip, with orifice directly in front.

Bay The voice of a hound that is on the trail.

Beard Whisker growth from under the chin.

B. of B. Best of Breed abbreviation.

Benched show A dog show where all dogs are benched on benches and secured to the bench by a collar and benching chain.

Bitch A female dog.

Bitchy Of male dog, over refined male or effeminate.

Bite The position of the lower and upper teeth when the mouth is closed.

Bladed bone Flat bone such as on the forelegs of the Borzoi.

Blaireau markings Grey and fawn with black shadings as seen in the Pyrenean Mountain Dogs.

Blanket Black saddle markings seen on Hounds.

133

Blaze A white line or marking that runs down the face from the skull to the muzzle.

Bloom Coat in top class condition with a lovely shine on it.

Blue belton Flecks of blue colour on white background. This particularly refers to English Setters that can be blue belton, lemon belton or orange belton.

Blue merle Blue and grey mixed (marbled effect) on a black coat as seen in Collies, Shetland Sheepdogs and Cardigan Corgis.

Bobtail Tail cut very short or docked as in Old English Sheepdogs.

Bone Strong limbs.

Bossy With too much muscular development of the shoulders.

Bow-legged With front legs sprung outward or hind legs too wide apart at the hocks and with the appearance of being 'bandy-legged'.

Brace Two dogs of the same breed.

Bracelets Rings of hair that are left on the legs of Poodles or Lowchens when they are in show clip.

Breeching Tan-coloured hair inside thighs as required in the Standards of Manchester and English Toy Terriers.

Brindle Mixture of black hairs with brown, tan or grey.

Brisket The part of the body in front of the chest and between the forelegs.

Broken-coated With wire-haired coat or a rough-textured coat, as in some Terriers.

Brush A bushy tail well covered by hair and like that of the fox.

Bull-necked With a neck that is too heavy or over-muscled.

Burr Inner formation of the ear.

Butterfly nose Part-coloured nose lacking pigmentation.

Buttocks Fleshy part of the upper thighs.

Button ears Semi-erect ears with the tip dropping forward close to the skull.

Canid Any animal belonging to the genus Canis which includes dogs, jackals and wolves. Adjective, canine.

Canine teeth The long teeth placed at the front corners of both upper and lower jaws and just behind the incisors.

Canter An easy gallop.

Cartilage Gristle. Tough flexible tissue acting as a lining to joints.

Castrate To remove surgically a dog's testicles.

Cat foot A foot that resembles that of a cat. A compact, tightly closed foot.

Challenge Certificate The Kennel Club award for the best of sex in a breed at a Championship Show which comes under their Rules and Regulations.

Champion A dog that has won three Challenge Certificates under three different judges in the UK. A dog that has won the required number of points in USA/Canada, Australia and European countries.

Character The make-up of a dog combining all essential points of appearance, disposition and behaviour.

Cheek Fleshy part of the head below the eyes and above the mouth.

Cheeky With rather thick, rounded and protruding cheeks.

Chest Area above the brisket and between the shoulder blades.

China eye A clear blue wall-eye.

Chiselled Clean cut in head with muzzle well modelled conforming to the breed standard.

Choke collar A chain or leather or nylon collar that loosens or tightens according to what is required by the handler.

Chops The lower cheeks, jaws, lips and mouth.

Clip The style in which a coat is presented.

Clipping When the dog moves his front legs are struck by his back feet and it gives a crablike action.

Cloddy Thick set and low and rather heavy.

Close-coupled Short from the last rib to hipbone, i.e. the loins.

Coarse Lacking quality and usually heavy in type.

Cobby Short and compact.

Collar White markings round the neck.

Condition General health, coat and appearance.

Conformation The general make-up of the dog structurally.

Corky Keen, with an alert expression.

Couple Two hounds.

Couples Fasteners coupling hounds together.

Couplings The loins.

Coursing When hounds hunt their quarry by sight.

Covering ground The amount of ground covered by an animal between forelegs and rear legs whilst on the move.

Cow-hocked Of a dog which bends his hocks inwards and his stifles and feet turn out. A serious fault.

Crabbing The dog moves sideways relative to the direction. The rear legs go past the front feet without clipping them.

Cranked tail A screw tail.

Crest Upper arched portion of neck. Hair on the head of a Chinese Crested Dog.

Cropping Trimming the ear leathers to stand erect instead of dropping forward. This surgical operation is not permitted in the UK.

Cross bred Resulting from a mating between two dogs of different breeds.

Croup The back immediately before the root of the tail.

Cryptorchid A male animal that does not have his testicles descended into the scrotum. When both testicles are affected the term bilateral cryptorchid is used and when only one testicle is affected the term unilateral cryptorchid is applied.

Cull To eliminate any unwanted whelps or dogs.

Culotte The long hair on the back of the thighs as in Schipperkes.

Cushion Padding or fullness of upper lips. Seen in Boxers and Bulldogs.

Dam The mother of a dog.

Dapple Mark with spots on a white or grey ground.

Daylight It is often said that there is too much daylight under a dog which means that it is too high on the leg.

Dentition The number and the arrangement of the teeth.

Dew claw Extra claw that is found on the inside of the lower portion of the legs. These are better removed a few days after birth.

135

Dewlap Rather loose pendulous skin found under the throat.

Dish face A concave muzzle as in a Pointer.

Down face An egg shaped outline to the head with no stop, as in the Bull Terrier.

Distemper teeth A discoloration of the teeth due to distemper or other virus.

Dock To shorten the tail surgically.

Dog The male member of the canine race.

Doggy Used to describe a bitch that is too masculine.

Double coat The outer coat should be weather-resistant with below a finer coat of softer, woolier hair which grows very near the skin and gives warmth.

Down in pasterns The front feet come forward at an angle instead of coming down in a fairly straight line from the forearm.

Drag An artificial line laid for hounds.

Drop ears Long, soft and pendulous ears hanging flat and close to the head.

Dry Free from any surplus skin or flesh around the mouth, lips and throat.

Dual Champion A dog that has not only qualified in the show ring but also for a Working Certificate as a gundog in the field. In America such a dog would be known as a 'bench and field Champion'.

Dudley nose Brown or light brown nose and quite distinct from a **Butterfly nose**

Ectropion Turning out of the eyelids.

Elbow The joint at the top of the forearm.

Elbows out Elbows that turn out from the body.

Entropion Turning in of the eyelids.

Even bite When teeth meet edge to edge.

Ewe neck A thin neck which has an insufficient, faulty or concave arch.

Expression A combination of the position of the eye, the colour and the size which gives the head the ideal or correct expression.

Fall Hair overhanging face.

False heat When a bitch appears to think she is in season and acts accordingly. This does not usually persist for any length of time and if the bitch is mated it usually proves unsuccessful.

Fang A large canine tooth.

Feathering Long hair fringe on ears, legs and tail.

Femur Thigh bone which extends from the hips to stifle joint.

Fiddle front Forelegs that are out at elbow with feet turned out.

Flag Long hair on the tail as in Setters.

Flank Side of body below the loins.

Flat-catcher A very flashy dog who because of his good showmanship hides his not-so-good points and many judges are deceived by this.

Flat-sided With very little spring of rib.

Flews Pendulous lips.

Flyer A very good exhibit of any breed.

Flying ears Ears that are carried to the side and not correctly folded.

Forearm The long bone of the front leg between the elbow and the pasterns.

Forechest Pad of muscle at the front of the chest.

Foreface Muzzle.

Forehand The front of the dog excluding the head.
Foreign expression An expression that is untypical of the breed.
Frill Long hair on chest and sides of neck.
Fringes Long hair on ears, tail and legs.
Front The forehand of the body, forelegs, chest, brisket and shoulders.
Furrow Line down centre of skull to stop.
Gait Leg action of the dog in movement.
Gay tail A tail that is carried higher than the standard demands—sometimes it can curl over the back.
Gaze hound A hound that hunts by sight rather than by scent.
Goose-rumped When the croup slopes away very sharply.
Grizzled With a mixture of black and grey hairs.
Gun-barrel front Absolutely straight front legs.
Hackney action When the front legs are lifted high in the manner of the Hackney horse.
Handler The person in charge of a dog in the show ring.
Hare foot A long narrow, oval foot.
Harlequin Black or blue patches on a white background as in Great Danes.
Harsh coat A stiff, wiry coat.
Haunch The area above the hips.
Haw The inner surface of the lower eyelid.
Hazel Light brown shade.
Heat The term to describe a bitch in season.
Height The measurement of the dog from the withers to the ground.
Herring-gutted Slab-sided.
Hock The joints in the hind legs between the pasterns and stifles.
Hocks well let down Hocks that are close to the ground.
Hound-marked The characteristic markings of Beagles, Harriers and Foxhounds.
Incisors The front teeth between the canine teeth.
Jaws The upper and lower part of the foreface where the teeth are placed.
Jowls Flesh of jaws and lips.
Keel Breastbone.
Kennel blindness The inability of a kennel owner to see faults in their own dogs and to see any virtues in other people's dogs.
Knuckling over This is caused by the front legs bulging over at the knee. See sometimes in Basset Hounds.
Lay back Receding nose. The placement of the shoulder—i.e. the scapula bone in relation to the withers.
Leathers Flap of the ear.
Leggy Legs that are too long for the dog and put it out of balance with the rest of the body.
Level bite When the teeth of the upper and lower incisors meet edge to edge.
Line breeding The mating of two dogs with similar strains but not too closely related.
Linty The texture of the coat of the Bedlington Terrier and the top-knot of the Dandie Dinmont Terrier.

137

Lippy When the lips overhang or are more developed than they should be.

Litter Puppies born at one whelping of the bitch.

Loaded shoulders A general heaviness of the shoulders usually caused by excessive muscle under and over the shoulder blade.

Loins The part of the body between the last rib and the hindquarters.

Low set When the tail is set lower or below the level of the topline.

Lower thigh Often referred to as second thigh. That part of the hindquarters from the stifle to the hock.

Lumber Too much flesh or muscle making the animal ungainly in appearance.

Lurcher A crossbred dog.

Maiden bitch A bitch that has not had a litter.

Mane Profuse hair growth on the neck.

Mask Shading on the foreface.

Mating The act by which a bitch is served in copulation by a dog, for the purpose of reproduction.

Merle A mixture of black/blue/grey colour.

Milk teeth The puppy teeth.

Molar One of the rear teeth which are used for grinding.

Molera This refers to Chihuahuas when the bones in the skull do not close in fully.

Mongrel A dog of mixed ancestry carrying the bloodlines of several pure-bred dogs of different breeds or of dogs with mixed parentage themselves.

Monorchid A male animal with only one testicle in the scrotum.

Muzzle The foreface in front of the eyes, i.e. nasal bone, nostril and jaws including mouth.

N.F.C. Not for Competition—refers to dogs entered at a show for display purposes only and not for any competition.

Neck The first seven vertebrae of spine from head to withers.

Nose A hound's scenting ability.

Nostril External opening of nose.

Occiput The upper back point of the skull.

Oestrum The menstrual period, that during which a bitch may be mated.

Olfactory Pertaining to the sense of smell.

Otter tail A thick-rooted round tapering tail, covered in thick strong hair with no feathering. As in an otter.

Out at elbow With elbows turned out from the body, standing or moving.

Out at shoulder With shoulder blades set rather widely and loosely.

Outcross When two dogs are mated that are unrelated.

Overshot When the front teeth project over and beyond the bottom teeth.

Pace A gait in which the legs move in lateral pairs, i.e. both legs on one side being moved before those on the other side.

Pack Several hounds kept together for the purpose of hunting as a team.

Pad The sole of the foot.

Paddling When the dog throws his front feet out sideways in a rather loose and uncontrolled manner. It makes the dog look wide in front on the move.

Particolour Patching with two or more colours; very often white is involved.

Pastern The lowest part of the front leg between the knee and the foot.

Patella A cap-like bone similar to the knee in man situated just above the stifle joint.

Pedigree A table of genealogy giving the ancestry of the dog.

Pelvis A cage-like set of bones formed by the pelvic arch and the adjoining bones.

Pencilling Black lines on the tan of the toes in black and tan breeds.

Period of gestation The time taken by a bitch to produce her litter. This is usually about sixty-three days.

Pied A term used for a coat that has two or three colours in the mixture.

Pig eye A very small rather deformed eye. As in a pig.

Pig jaw An overshot jaw.

Pigeon-toed When the forefeet incline inwards towards each other.

Pile Thick undercoat of soft hair.

Pincer bite Front teeth meeting edge to edge.

Pin toes Toes pointing inwards.

Pipe-stopper tail A long thin tail with no substance in it.

Plume Long hair on the tail of breeds that carry their tail over their back, e.g. Elkhound, Keeshond.

Point of shoulder Joint between the shoulder and the upper arm.

Points Colour on face, ears, legs and tail. May be white, black or tan.

Pompon Rounded tuft of hair left on the tail when the coat is clipped as in the poodle.

Prefix Attached to the front of a dog's name, it indicates the kennel from where it has come.

Premolar teeth The small teeth that are placed between the large back teeth and the large canine teeth.

Pricked ear Ears that are carried erect and are usually pointed at the tip.

Puppy A dog that does not exceed twelve months of age.

Quality An over-all general excellence of character, expression and conformation, standing and moving.

Quarters The hindquarters.

Racy Rather slight in build with long legs and body, giving an impression of speed.

Rangy Tall and long in body and rather loose-limbed but with greater substance than one that is racy.

Rat tail A thin tail that has short smooth hair.

Reachy Covering a lot of ground between the front and hind feet.

Ribbed up Compact, with well-sprung ribs.

Rickets A disease of the bone usually caused by bad rearing.

Ring The area in which a judge assesses the dogs at a show.

Ring tail Carried high up and round, almost in a circle.

Roached back A dog with a marked curve in his back from the withers over the loin and down to the croup.

Roan A fine mixture of coloured hair with white hair as seen in Cocker Spaniels.

Roman nose Nose of which the tip turns down and back

Rose ear A small drop ear folding over and back and showing the burr.

Ruff Thick, long hair around the neck.

Sabre tail Carried in a semi-circle.

Sable Black hair intermingled with a lighter ground colour such as in Collies.

Saddle Black markings over back like a saddle. Seen in hounds.

Saddle-backed Sway backed (q.v.).

Scapula The shoulder blade.

Scent The odour given off by a quarry.

Scissor bite When the incisors of the upper jaw just overlap the ones on the bottom jaw.

Screw tail A tail that is twisted or screwed.

Scrotum Bag of skin that holds the testicles.

Season A term for a bitch during the period of her oestrum.

Second thigh The lower thigh.

Self colour One colour or whole colour with or without lighter shading.

Semi-erect ear Pricked ear with tip just falling slightly over as in Collies.

Septum The very thin dividing bone between the nostrils.

Service The term given to the mating of a bitch with the dog.

Set-on Where the root of the tail meets the body.

Shelly Lacking bone and substance throughout.

Short-coupled Short and strong in the loins.

Shoulder The point at which the height of a dog is measured and it is created by the shoulder blade and the muscles that support it.

Sickle hock When the hocks are so bent that the part below the hock joint is placed forward and is not vertical.

Sickle tail A tail carried high in a semi-circle.

Sire The male parent of a litter.

Skully Thick and coarse across the skull.

Slab-sided With flat sides and little or no spring of ribs.

Sloping shoulders Those that are well laid back and capable of allowing the dog to move with scope.

Snipey With a weak, narrow muzzle.

Spaying A surgical operation to prevent the bitch from conceiving.

Spectacles Shadings or dark markings around the eyes as in Keeshonds.

Spine Vertebral column along back that sustains the frame.

Splashes White markings on a solid colour.

Splay foot A foot with loose, badly fitting toes that are spread wide apart.

Squirrel tail A tail that comes forward and lies almost flat on the back.

Standard The official description of the breed to which dogs should be judged.

Stern The tail of a hound.

Sternum The breast bone.

Stifle The joint in the hind leg between the thigh and the second thigh.

Stilted With a choppy, restricted gait usually caused by upright shoulders and straight stifles.

Stop The depression between the eyes and dividing the forehead and the muzzle.

Straight shoulders Insufficient angulation between shoulder blade and upper arm.

Substance Good bone, body weight and power, throughout.

Sway back Dipping of the topline between withers and hipbones.

Team Three or more of one breed shown together.

Tendon Band of tough tissue connecting muscle to bone.

Terrier front Straight up-and-down profile. Short upper arm, showing little or no forechest.

Texture Nature of coat.

Thorax The ribcage and its contents.

Throat Part of neck that comes below the lower jaw.

Throaty Too much loose skin under the throat.

Thumb mark Black spots on pasterns as in Manchester Terriers.

Ticked Comparatively small areas of coloured hair in a white coat or undercoat.

Timber Bone, especially of the legs.

Tongue When hounds give voice when they are on the scent.

Topknot Tuft of hair on the top of the head.

Topline Profile of dog from occiput to tail base.

Trace Dark line along the back as seen in Pugs.

Tricolour Black, white and tan.

Trunk The body.

Tuck-up Upward curve under the belly of a dog.

Turn-up An uptilted under jaw as in the bulldog.

Type Distinguishing breed characteristics as given in the Breed Standard.

Undercoat Soft, short hair concealed by longer coat.

Undershot Having the lower incisors projected beyond the upper incisors.

Upper arm The humerus, which is the bone of the foreleg between the shoulder blade and forearm.

Upright shoulder Insufficient angulation of the shoulder blade.

Vent The area that immediately surrounds the anus.

Wall-eye Blue eye.

Weaving The front legs cross when in action.

Weedy Lightly formed and lacking bone and substance.

Well let down With correct degree of angulation of stifle and hock joint.

Well sprung Having rounded and well formed ribs.

Wheaten Pale yellow or fawn in colour.

Whelp A very young puppy.

Whelping The act of giving birth to puppies.

Whip tail A rather stiffly carried tail that is straight and pointed and carried horizontally.

Whiskers Long hairs on chin and muzzle.

Wire-haired With coat of rough wiry texture.

Withers Highest part of the body just behind the neck and where the top of the shoulder blades may be felt.

Wrinkle Loose skin on the forehead and/or face.

141

Wry jaw When the lower jaw is tilted from one side to another and is not parallel with the upper jaw. Although it is usually the lower jaw that is the culprit the upper jaw can be affected.

Appendices

List of recognized breeds: UK

Listed below are the 124 breeds that are recognized by the Kennel
Club, and also other breeds which, perhaps for want of a better
name, are known as Rare Breeds in Britain. This means that these
latter breeds do not, as yet, have enough registrations and/or entries
at shows to warrant the granting of Challenge Certificates by the
Kennel Club. They are usually entered in the Non-Classified Classes
but at the larger shows they may have their own separate breed
classes. For identification purposes I have listed these Rare Breeds
in their Group marked with an asterisk.

Sporting Breeds

Hound Group
Afghans, Basenjis, Bassets, Basset Griffons Vendeen*, Beagles,
Bloodhounds, Borzois, Dachshunds Long Hair, Dachshunds
Miniature Long Hair, Dachshunds Smooth Hair, Dachshunds
Miniature Smooth Hair, Dachshunds Wire Hair, Dachshunds
Miniature Wire Hair, Deerhounds, Elkhounds, Finnish Spitz,
Foxhounds*, Greyhounds, Ibizan Hounds, Irish Wolfhounds,
Otterhounds*, Pharaoh Hounds, Portuguese Warren Hounds*,
Rhodesian Ridgebacks, Salukis, Sloughis*, Swedish Foxhounds*,
Whippets.

Gundog Group
Brittany Spaniels*, English Setters, German Shorthaired Pointers,
German Longhaired Pointers*, German Wirehaired Pointers*,
Gordon Setters, Hungarian Vizslas, Irish Setters, Large
Munsterlanders, Pointers, Retrievers Chesapeake Bay*, Retrievers
Curly Coated, Retrievers Flat Coated, Retrievers Golden, Retrievers
Labrador, Spaniels American Cocker, Spaniels Clumber, Spaniels
Cocker, Spaniels English Springer, Spaniels Field, Spaniels Irish
Water, Spaniels Sussex, Spaniels Welsh Springer, Weimaraners.

Terrier Group
Airedales, Australians, Bedlingtons, Borders, Bull Terriers, Bull Terriers Miniature, Cairns, Kerry Blue Terriers, Lakelands, Manchesters, Norfolk, Norwich, Scottish Terriers, Sealyham Terriers, Dandie Dinmont Terriers, Fox Terriers Smooth, Fox Terriers Wire, Glen of Imal Terriers*, Irish Terriers, Skye Terriers, Soft Coated Wheaten Terriers, Staffordshire Bull Terriers, Welsh Terriers, West Highland White Terriers.

Non-Sporting Breeds

Utility Group
Bostons, Bulldogs, Chow Chows, Dalmatians, French Bulldogs, Japanese Akitas*, Keeshonds, Leonbergers*, Lhasa Apsos, Miniature Schnauzers, Poodles Standard, Poodles Miniature, Poodles Toy, Schipperkes, Schnauzers, Shih Tzus, Tibetan Spaniels, Tibetan Terriers.

Working Group
Alaskan Malamutes*, Anatolian Sheepdogs*, Australian Kelpies*, Bearded Collies, Belgian Shepherd Dogs (Groenendaels), Belgian Shepherd Dogs (Malinois)*, Belgian Shepherd Dogs (Tervuerens), Bernese Mountain Dogs, Bouviers Des Flandres*, Boxers, Briards, Bullmastiffs, Collies Rough, Collies Smooth, Dobermanns, Estrela Mountain Dogs*, Giant Schnauzers, Great Danes, Hungarian Kuvasz*, Hungarian Pulis, Huskies*, Hungarian Komondors*, German Shepherd Dogs (Alsatians), Maremma Sheepdogs, Mastiffs, Neapolitan Mastiffs*, Newfoundlands, Norwegian Buhunds, Old English Sheepdogs, Portuguese Water Dogs*, Pyrenean Mountain Dogs, Rottweilers, St Bernards, Samoyeds, Shetland Sheepdogs, Siberian Huskies*, Swedish Vallhunds*, Tibetan Mastiffs*, Welsh Corgis Cardigan, Welsh Corgis Pembroke.

Toy Group
Affenpinschers*, Australian Silky Terriers*, Bichon Frise, Cavalier King Charles Spaniels, Chihuahuas Long Coat, Chihuahuas Smooth Coat, Chinese Crested Dogs, English Toy Terriers, Griffons, Italian Greyhounds, Japanese Chin, King Charles Spaniels, Lowchen, Maltese, Miniature Pinschers, Papillons, Pekingese, Pomeranians, Pugs, Yorkshire Terriers.

Docking

For the following breeds, docking is a requirement or option in the official standards:
German Shorthaired Pointers, Hungarian Vizslas, Large Munsterlanders (docking optional), American Cockers, Clumbers, Cocker Spaniels, English Springers, Field Spaniels, Sussex Spaniels, Welsh Springers, Weimaraners, All Schnauzers, All Poodles, Airedale Terriers, Australian Terriers, Fox Terriers, Smooth and Wire, Irish Terriers, Kerry Blue Terriers, Lakeland Terriers, Norfolk Terriers, Norwich Terriers, Scottish Terriers, Sealyham Terriers, Soft Coated Wheaten Terriers, Welsh Terriers, West Highland White Terriers, Bouviers Des Flandres, Boxers, Dobermanns, Old English Sheepdogs (if required), Rottweilers, Swedish Vallhunds, Pembroke Corgis, Affenpinschers (docking optional), Cavalier King Charles (docking optional), Griffons, Miniature Pinschers, Yorkshire Terriers.

List of recognized breeds: USA

The American Kennel Club groups the breeds as follows:

Group I – Sporting Dogs

Pointers German Shorthaired, Pointers German Wirehaired, Retrievers Chesapeake Bay, Retrievers Curly Coated, Retrievers Flat Coated, Retrievers Golden, Retrievers Labrador, Setters English, Setters Gordon, Setters Irish, Spaniels American Water, Spaniels Brittany, Spaniels Clumber, Spaniels Cocker, Spaniels English Cocker, Spaniels English Springer, Spaniels Field, Spaniels Irish Water, Spaniels Sussex, Spaniels Welsh Springer, Vizslas, Weimaraners, Wirehaired Pointing Griffons.

Group II – Hounds

Afghan Hounds, Basenjis, Basset Hounds, Beagles, Black and Tan Coonhounds, Bloodhounds, Borzois, Dachshunds, Foxhounds American, Foxhounds English, Greyhounds, Harriers, Ibizan Hounds, Irish Wolfhounds, Norwegian Elkhounds, Otter Hounds, Rhodesian Ridgebacks, Salukis, Scottish Deerhounds, Whippets.

With effect from 1 January 1983 Group III will be split into two as follows:

Working Group

Akitas, Alaskan Malamutes, Bernese Mountain Dogs, Boxers, Bullmastiffs, Dobermann Pinschers, Giant Schnauzers, Great Danes, Great Pyrenees, Komondors, Kuvaszs, Mastiffs, Newfoundlands, Rottweilers, St Bernards, Samoyeds, Siberian Huskies, Standard Schnauzers.

Herding Group

Australian Cattle Dogs, Bearded Collies, Belgian Shepherd Dogs

(Groenendaels), Belgian Shepherd Dogs (Malinois), Belgian Shepherd Dogs (Terveren), Bouviers des Flandres, Briards, Collies, German Shepherd Dogs, Old English Sheepdogs, Pulis, Shetland Sheepdogs, Welsh Corgi Cardigans, Welsh Corgi Pembrokes.

Group IV – Terriers

Airedale Terriers, American Staffordshire Terriers, Australian Terriers, Bedlington Terriers, Border Terriers, Bull Terriers, Cairn Terriers, Dandie Dinmont Terriers, Fox Terriers, Irish Terriers, Kerry Blue Terriers, Lakeland Terriers, Manchester Terriers, Miniature Schnauzers, Norfolk Terriers, Norwich Terriers, Scottish Terriers, Sealyham Terriers, Skye Terriers, Soft Coated Wheaten Terriers, Staffordshire Bull Terriers, Welsh Terriers, West Highland White Terriers.

Group V – Toys

Affenpinschers, Brussels Griffons, Chihuahuas, English Toy Spaniels, Italian Greyhounds, Japanese Spaniels, Maltese, Manchester Terriers (Toy), Miniature Pinschers, Papillons, Pekingese, Pomeranians, Poodles (Toy), Pugs, Shih Tzus, Silky Terriers, Yorkshire Terriers.

Group VI – Non Sporting Dogs

Bichon Frises, Boston Terriers, Bulldogs, Chow Chows, Dalmatians, French Bulldogs, Keeshonds, Lhasa Apsos, Poodles, Schipperkes, Tibetan Terriers.

Cruft's Best in Show winners 1928–1982

Before 1928 there was no award of Best in Show at Cruft's. Since that time the following dogs have gained this award:

1928 Greyhound, Primely Sceptre – H. Whitley
1929 Scottish Terrier, Heather Necessity, E. Chapman
1930 Spaniel (Cocker), Luckystar of Ware, H. S. Lloyd
1931 Spaniel (Cocker), Luckystar of Ware, H. S. Lloyd
1932 Retriever (Labrador), Branshaw Bob, Lorna Countess Howe
1933 Retriever (Labrador), Branshaw Bob, Lorna Countess Howe
1934 Greyhound, Southball Moonstone, B. Hartland Worden
1935 Pointer, Pennine Prima Donna, A. Eggleston
1936 Chow Chow, Ch. Choonam Hung Kwong, Mrs V. A. M. Mannooch
1937 Retriever (Labrador), Ch. Cheveralla Ben of Banchory, Lorna Countess Howe
1938 Spaniel (Cocker), Exquisite Model of Ware, H. S. Lloyd
1939 Spaniel (Cocker), Exquisite Model of Ware, H. S. Lloyd
1948 Spaniel (Cocker), Tracy Witch of Ware, H. S. Lloyd
1950 Spaniel (Cocker), Tracy Witch of Ware, H. S. Lloyd
1951 Welsh Terrier, Twynstar Dyma – Fl. Capt and Mrs Thomas
1952 Bulldog, Ch. Noways Chuckles – J. T. Barnard
1953 Great Dane, Ch. Elch Elder of Ouborough, W. G. Siggers
1954 Cancelled
1955 Poodle (Standard), Ch. Tzigane Aggri of Nashend, Mrs A. Proctor
1956 Greyhound, Treetops Golden Falcon, Mrs W. de Casembroot and Miss H. Greenich
1957 Keeshond, Ch. Vollrijk of Vorden, Mrs I. M. Tucker
1958 Pointer, Ch. Chiming Bells, Mrs W. Parkinson
1959 Welsh Terrier, Ch. Sandstorm Saracen, Mesdames Leach and Thomas
1960 Irish Wolfhound, Sulhamstead Merman, Mrs Nagle and Miss Clark

1961 Airedale Terrier, Ch. Riverina Tweedsbairn, Miss P. McCaughey and Mrs D. Schuth

1962 Fox Terrier (Wire), Ch. Crackwyn Cockspur, H. L. Gill

1963 Lakeland Terrier, Rogerholm Recruit, W. Rogers

1964 English Setter, Sh. Ch. Silbury Soames of Maida Vale, Mrs Williams

1965 Alsatian (GSD), Ch. Fenton of Kentwood, Miss S. Godden

1966 Poodle (Toy), Oakington Puckshill Amber Sunblush, Mrs C. Perry

*1967 Lakeland Terrier, Ch. Stingray of Derryabah, Mr and Mrs W. Postlewaite

1968 Dalmatian, Ch. Fanhill Faune, Mrs J. Woodyatt

1969 Alsatian (GSD), Ch. Hendrawen's Nibelung of Charavigne, Mr and Mrs E. J. White

1970 Pyrenean Mountain Dog, Bergerie Knur, Mr and Mrs F. S. Prince

1971 Alsatian (GSD), Ch. Ramacon Swashbuckler, Prince Ahmed Hussain

1972 Bull Terrier, Ch. Abraxas Audacity, Miss Drummond Dick

1973 Cavalier King Charles Spaniel, Alansmere Aquarius, Messrs. Hall and Evans

1974 St Bernard, Ch. Burtonswood Bossy Boots, Miss M. Hindes

1975 Fox Terrier (Wire) Ch. Brookewire Brandy of Layven, Messrs Benelli and Dondina

1976 West Highland White Terrier, Ch. Dianthus Buttons, Mrs K. Newstead

1977 English Setter, Bournehouse Dancing Master,* Mr G. F. Williams

1978 Fox Terrier (Wire), Ch. Harrowhill Huntsman, Miss E. Hnowles

1979 Kerry Blue Terrier, Eng. American Ch. Callaghan of Leander, Mrs W. Streatfield

1980 Retriever (Flat-Coated), Ch. Shargleam Blackcap, Miss P. Chapman

1981 Irish Setter, Ch. Astley's Portia of Rua, Miss and Mrs Tuite

1982 Toy Poodle, Ch. Grayco Hazelnut, Mrs Lesley Howard

* The Lakeland Terrier who won Cruft's in 1967 was sold to America and won Best in Show at Westminster in 1968 – Ch. Stingray of Derryabah.

Westminster Kennel Club (New York) Best in Show Winners 1907–1982

1907 Winthrop Rutherford–Ch. Warren Remedy, Smooth Fox Terrier

1908 Winthrop Rutherford–Ch. Warren Remedy, Smooth Fox Terrier

1909 Winthrop Rutherford–Ch. Warren Remedy, Smooth Fox Terrier

1910 Sabine Kennels–Ch. Sabine Rarebit, Smooth Fox Terrier

1911 A. Albright Jr.–Ch. Tickle Em Jock, Scottish Terrier

1912 William P. Wolcott–Ch. Kenmare Sorceress, Airedale Terrier

1913 Alex H. Stewart–Ch. Strathtay Prince Albert, Bulldog

1914 Mrs Tylor Morse–Ch. Slumber, Old English Sheepdog

1915 George W. Quintard–Ch. Matford Vic, Wire Fox Terrier

1916 George W. Quintard–Ch. Matford Vic, Wire Fox Terrier

1917 Mrs Roy A. Rainey–Ch. Conejo Wycollar Boy, Wire Fox Terrier

1918 R. H. Elliott–Ch. Haymarket Faultless, Bull Terrier

1919 G. L. Davis–Ch. Briergate Bright Beauty, Airedale Terrier

1920 Mrs Roy A. Rainey–Ch. Conejo Wycollar Boy, Wire Fox Terrier

1921 William T. Payne–Ch. Midkiff Seductive, Cocker Spaniel

1922 Frederic C. Hodd–Ch. Boxwood Barkentine, Airedale Terrier

1923 There was no Best in Show award in this year

1924 Bayard Warren–Ch. Barberryhill Bootlegger, Sealyham Terrier

1925 Robert F. Maloney–Ch. Governor Moscow, Pointer

1926 Halleston Kennels–Ch. Signal Circuit of Halleston, Wire Fox Terrier

1927 Frederic C. Brown–Ch. Pinegrade Perfection, Sealyham Terrier

1928 R. M. Lewis–Ch. Talavera Margaret, Wire Fox Terrier

1929 Mrs Florence B. Lich–Laund Loyalty of Bellhaven, Collie

1930 John G. Bates–Ch. Pendley Calling of Blarney, Wire Fox Terrier

1931 John G. Bates–Ch. Pendley Calling of Blarney, Wire Fox Terrier

1932 Giralda Farms – Ch. Nancolleth Markable, Pointer
1933 S. M. Stewart – Ch. Warland Protector of Shelterock, Airedale
Terrier
1934 Halleston Kennels – Ch. Flornell Spicy Bit of Halleston, Wire
Fox Terrier
1935 Blakeen Kennels – Ch. Nunsoe Duc de la Terrace of Blakeen,
Standard Poodle
1936 Claredale Kennels – Ch. St. Margaret Magnificent of Claredale,
Sealyham Terrier
1937 Halleston Kennels – Ch. Flornell Spicy Piece of Halleston, Wire
Fox Terrier
1938 Maridor Kennels – Ch. Daro of Maridor, English Setter
1939 Giralda Farms – Ch. Ferry v. Rauhfelsen of Giralda, Dobermann
1940 H. E. Mellenthin – Ch. My Own Brucie, Cocker Spaniel
1941 H. E. Mellenthin – Ch. My Own Brucie, Cocker Spaniel
1942 Mrs J. G. Winant – Ch. Wolvey Pattern of Edgerstoune, West
Highland White Terrier
1943 Mrs P. H. B. Frelinghuysen – Ch. Pitter Patter of Piperscroft,
Miniature Poodle
1944 Mrs Edward P. Alker – Ch. Flornell Rare Bit of Twin Ponds,
Welsh Terrier
1945 Mr and Mrs T. H. Snethen – Ch. Shieling's Signature, Scottish
Terrier
1946 Mr and Mrs T. H. Carruthers III – Ch. Heatherington Model
Rhythm, Wire Fox Terrier
1947 Mr and Mrs Richard C. Kettles, Jr. – Ch. Warlord of Mazelaine,
Boxer
1948 Mr and Mrs William A. Rockefeller – Ch. Rock Ridge Night
Rocket, Bedlington Terrier
1949 Mr and Mrs John Phelps Wagner – Ch. Mazelaine Zazarac
Brandy, Boxer
1950 Mrs J. G. Winant – Ch. Walsing Winning Trick of Edgerstoune,
Scottish Terrier
1951 Dr and Mrs R. C. Harris – Ch. Bang Away of Sirrah Crest, Boxer
1952 Mr and Mrs Len Carey – Ch. Rancho Dobe's Storm,
Dobermann
1953 Mr and Mrs Len Carey – Ch. Rancho Dobe's Storm,
Dobermann
1954 Mrs Carl E. Morgan – Ch. Carmor's Rise and Shine, Cocker
Spaniel

1955 John A. Saylor MD – Ch. Kippax Fearnought, Bulldog

1956 Bertha Smith – Ch. Wilber White Swan, Toy Poodle

1957 Sunny Shay and Dorothy Chenade – Ch. Shirkhan of Grandeur, Afghan Hound

1958 Puttencove Kennels – Ch. Puttencove Promise, Standard Poodle

1959 Dunwalke Kennels – Ch. Fontclair Festoon, Miniature Poodle

1960 Mr and Mrs C. C. Venable – Ch. Chik T'Sun of Caversham, Pekingese

1961 Miss Florence Michelson – Ch. Cappoquin Little Sister, Toy Poodle

1962 Wishing Well Kennels – Ch. Elfinbrook Simon, West Highland White Terrier

1963 Mrs W. J. S. Borie – Ch. Wakefield's Black Knight, English Springer

1964 Pennyworth Kennels – Ch. Courtenay Fleetfoot of Pennyworth, Whippet

1965 Mr and Mrs Charles C. Stalter – Ch. Carmichaels Fanfare, Scottish Terrier

1966 Marion G. Bunker – Ch. Zeloy Mooremaide's Magic, Wire Fox Terrier

1967 E. H. Stuart – Ch. Bardene Bingo, Scottish Terrier

1968 Mr and Mrs James A. Farrell Jr. – Ch. Stingray of Derryabah, Lakeland Terrier

1969 Walter F. Goodman and Mrs Adele F. Goodman – Ch. Glamoor Good News, Skye Terrier

1970 Dr and Mrs P. J. Pagano and Dr Theodore S. Fickes – Ch. Arriba's Prima Donna, Boxer

1971 Milton E. Prickett – Ch. Chinoe's Adamant James, English Springer Spaniel

1972 Milton E. Prickett – Ch. Chinoe's Adamant James, English Springer Spaniel

1973 Edward B. Jenner and Jo Anne Scring – Ch. Acadia Command Performance, Standard Poodle

1974 Richard P. Smith MD – Ch. Gretchenhof Columbia River, German Shorthaired Pointer

1975 Mr and Mrs Vanword – Ch. Sir Lancelot of Barvan, Old English Sheepdog

1976 Mrs V. K. Dickson – Ch. Jo Ni's Red Baron of Crofton, Lakeland Terrier

1977 Pool Forge Kennels – Ch. Dersade Bobby's Girl, Sealyham Terrier
1978 Barbara A. and Charles W. Switzer – Ch. Cede Higgins, Yorkshire Terrier
1979 Mrs Anne E. Snelling – Ch. Oak Tree's Irishtocrat, Irish Water Spaniel
1980 Kathleen Kanzler – Ch. Innisfree's Sierra Cinnar, Siberian Husky
1981 Robert A. Hausiohner – Ch. Dhandys Favorite Woodchuck, Pug
1982 Mrs Anne E. Snelling – Ch St Aubry Dragonora of Elsdon, Pekingese

Kennel Clubs worldwide: names and addresses

Australia
Australian National Kennel Council—Royal Show Grounds, Ascot
    Vale, Victoria
Incorporating: The Canine Association of Western Australia
N. Australian Canine Association
The Canine Control Council (Queensland)
Canberra Kennel Association
The Kennel Control Council
Kennel Control Council of Tasmania
The RAS Kennel Club
South Australian Canine Association

Barbados
Barbados Kennel Club, Wraysbury, Bucks, St. Thomas, Barbados,
    W.I.

Belgium
Société Royale Saint-Hubert, Avenue de l'Armée 25, B-1040,
    Brussels, Belgium

Bermuda
The Bermuda Kennel Club Inc., PO Box 1455, Hamilton 5,
    Bermuda

Brazil
Brazil Kennel Club, Caixa Postal, 1468, Rio de Janeiro

Burma
Burma Kennel Club

Canada
Canadian Kennel Club, 2150 Bloor Street West, Toronto M6S 1M8,
    Ontario

Caribbean
The Caribbean Kennel Club, PO Box 737, Port of Spain, Trinidad

Chile
Kennel Club de Chile, Casilla 1704, Valparaiso

Colombia
Club Canino Colombiano, Calle 70, No 4-60, 3er Piso, Bogota, D.E.
  Colombia

Denmark
Dansk Kennelklub, Parkvej 1, Jersie Strand, 2680, Solrad Strand

East Africa
East Africa Kennel Club, PO Box 14223, Westlands, Nairobi,
  Kenya, E. Africa

Finland
Suomen Kennelliitto-Finska Kennelklubben, Bulevardi 14A,
  Helsinki

France
Société Centrale Canine, 215 Rue St Denis, 75083 Paris, Cedex 02

Germany
Verband für das Deutsche Hundewesen (VDH), Postfach 1390, 46
  Dortmund

Great Britain
The Kennel Club, 1 Clarges Street, Piccadilly, London W1Y 8AB

Guernsey
Guernsey Dog Club, Myrtle Grove, St. Jacques, Guernsey, C.I.

Holland
Raad van Beheer op Kynologisch Gebied in Nederland, Emmalaan
  16, Amsterdam

Hong Kong
Hong Kong Kennel Club, 3rd Floor, 28B Stanley Street, Hong
  Kong

India
Kennel Club of India, Kenhope, Coonoor I, Nilgiris, S. India

Ireland
Irish Kennel Club, 23 Earlsfort Terrace, Dublin 2

Italy
Ente Nazionale Della Cinofilia Italiana, Viale Premuda, 21 Milan

Jamaica
The Jamaican Kennel Club, 8 Orchard Street, Kingston 5, Jamaica,
W.I.

Jersey
Jersey Dog Club, Coburg House, Rue-es-Picots, Trinity, Jersey,
C.I.

Malaysia
Malaysian Kennel Association, PO Box 303, Julan Sultan, Petaling,
Jaya, Selangor, Malaysia

Malta GC
Main Kennel Club c/o Msida Youth Centre, 15 Rue d'Argens Str,
Msida, Malta G.C.

Monaco
Société Canine de Monaco, Palais des Congrès, Avenue d'Ostende,
Monte Carlo

Nepal
Nepal Kennel Club, PO Box 653, Kathmandu, Nepal

New Zealand
New Zealand Kennel Club, Private Bag, Porirua, New Zealand

Norway
Norsk Kennelklub, Teglverksgt 8, Rodelokka, Postboks 6598, Oslo 5

Pakistan
The Kennel Club of Pakistan, 17a Khayaban-I-Iqbal, Shalimar 7,
Islamabad, Pakistan

Portugal
Cluba Portuguese de Canicultura, Praca D. Joao da Camara 4-3,
  Lisbon 2

Singapore
The Singapore Kennel Club, 275-F Selegie Complex, Selegie Road,
  Singapore 7

South Africa
Kennel Union of Southern Africa, 6th Floor, Bree Castle, 68 Bree
  Street, Cape Town 8001, S. Africa—PO Box 11280, Vlaeberg
  8018, S. Africa

Spain
Real Sociedad Central de Fomento de las Razas en Espana, Los
  Madrazo 20, Madrid 14

Sweden
Svenska Kennelklubben, Norrbyvagan 30, Box 11043, 161 11
  Bromma, Sweden

Switzerland
Schweizerische Kynologische Gesellschaft, Falkenplatz 11, 3012
  Berne, Switzerland

Uruguay
Kennel Club Uruguayo, Avda, Uruguay 864, Montevideo, South
  America

USA
American Kennel Club, 51 Madison Avenue, New York, NY 10010

Index

Index